LOST GLASGOW

*

GLASGOW'S LOST ARCHITECTURAL HERITAGE

Carol Foreman

BIRLINN

First published in 2002 by
Birlinn Limited
West Newington House
10 Newington Road
Edinburgh
EH9 1QS

www.birlinn.co.uk

Reprinted 2007,2009

ISBN : 978 1 84158 278 8

British Library Cataloguing-in-Publication Data
A catalogue record for this book is available
from the British Library.

Layout: Mark Blackadder

Printed and bound by Cromwell Press Group, Trowbridge

LOST
GLASGOW

*

To Iain Paterson
with thanks for his help and patience
in answering my many queries

CONTENTS

✳

GLASGOW*

*

Glasgow to Thee thy Neighbouring Towns give place,
'Bove them thou lifts thine head with comely grace.
Scarce in the spacious Earth can any see
A City that's more beautiful than thee.
Towards the setting Sun thou'rt built, and finds
The temperate breathings of the Western Winds.

More pure than Amber is the River Clyde,
Whose Gentle streams do by thy Borders glyde;
And here a thousand Sail receive commands
To traffick for thee unto Forraign Lands.

The buildings high and glorious are; yet be
More fair within than they are outwardly.
Thy Houses by thy Temples are outdone,
Thy glittering Temples of the fairest Stone:
And yet the Stones of them however fair
The Workmanship exceeds which is more rare.

That Neptune and Apollo did (it's said)
Troy's fam'd Walls rear and their foundations laid.
But thee, O Glasgow! we may justly deem
That all the Gods who have been in esteem,
Which in the Earth and Air and Ocean are,
Have joyn'd to build with a Propitious Star.

*from epigrams of Arthur Johnstoun, doctor of medcin upon some of our chief burghs, translated into english by I. B. 1685

INTRODUCTION

*

While *Lost Glasgow* deals principally with Glasgow's lost architectural heritage from medieval times to the end of the Victorian age, interwoven is the story of how the city evolved and how major events throughout the centuries affected its people, trade and environment. The area covered by *Lost Glasgow* is roughly that contained within the inner ring road (the M8 north of the Clyde), and buildings are grouped as to when they were built, not when they were demolished, allowing the history of the city to unfold. This would not have been possible if the buildings had been arranged in the order in which they were demolished, as most of 'Old Glasgow' vanished in Victorian times and most of the Victorian buildings that have been lost were destroyed in the second half of the twentieth century.

As Glasgow has lost so much of its architectural heritage, it has been very difficult to decide which buildings to include in *Lost Glasgow*. Consequently, there are probably many important buildings known to readers that have been omitted. For this, I apologise.

For the loss of so many of its historic buildings, Glasgow has only itself to blame. It has never been sentimental about its old buildings. It has been a point of civic pride to destroy and build better, and if old buildings got in the way of any new plan, they were swept away, supposedly in the name of progress. All that is left of the medieval city are the Cathedral and Provand's Lordship (1471), just one of the thirty-two prebendal manses that existed around the Cathedral. The only other relics of ancient Glasgow are three seventeenth-century steeples, the Tolbooth (1626), at the foot of High Street, the Tron (1636), in Trongate, and the Merchants (1665) in Bridgegate.

Although the Georgians expanded the city outside its medieval boundaries, they unforgivably allowed the Bishop's Castle to become a ruin and let the Cathedral fall into disrepair. They also destroyed the fifteenth-century St Nicholas Hospital and the seventeenth-century Tolbooth, Hutchesons' Hospital and Merchants House. The historic Shawfield Mansion, one of the earliest examples of a Palladian villa in Britain, disappeared in 1795 to make way for Glassford Street.

The disintegration of 'Old Glasgow' began in Victorian times with the pioneering City Improvement Act of 1866, which set up an Improvement Trust to clear and redevelop 90 acres in the notorious slum localities around Trongate, Saltmarket, Gallowgate and High Street. Included were parts of Calton and the Gorbals. The designated area had a population of over 50,000. The railway companies also did their bit, as their viaducts and bridges swept through the heart of the historic city, tearing down seventeenth-century houses in the Bridgegate. The Union Railway Scheme alone demolished over thirteen hundred houses when it ran its lines through Gallowgate, Saltmarket, Bridgegate and Glasgow Cross, with the Improvement Trustees paying for the widening of spans to allow for more spacious street layouts.

The Trustees of the Glasgow Improvement Scheme had the wisdom to commission Thomas Annan to make a photographic record of the old streets, wynds, vennels and closes before they were cleared. Three editions of *The Old Closes and Streets of Glasgow* were published between 1868 and 1900; the last edition included photographs taken after Annan's death in 1887. As the work of the Trust continued into the twentieth century, each edition had a different set of photographs.

Before the age of photography, illustrations by people like Joseph Swan, Andrew Donaldson, Thomas Fairbairn, William Simpson and David Small gave a wide-ranging idea of the city in the nineteenth century. Many of these illustrations appear in *Lost Glasgow*, as do maps showing the layout of the city through the ages.

As a matter of interest, no pictures of Glasgow exist before the end of the seventeenth century. Captain John Abraham Slezer, a Dutch soldier who came to Scotland in the 1660s and 1670s to help with military arrangements during the Covenanting troubles, was responsible for the first. While he moved about Scotland, he sketched many of the 'interesting prospects' he saw, but, as his sketches were not good enough for publication, after a visit to his native land he brought back a skilled 'prospect' painter, who drew 57 large views that were published in a volume called *Theatrum Scotiae* in London in 1693. Three of the scenes were of Glasgow – a view from the Merchants' Hill (the site of the Necropolis), a view of the south riverfront, apparently from Govanhill, and a view of the College and Blackfriars Church.

Although portrayed as ruthless vandals who destroyed almost all of Glasgow's old town and its Georgian buildings, in essence the Victorians were trying to improve the city, as by the middle of the nineteenth century the old town had become a vice-ridden overcrowded slum where cholera and typhus raged. Where they went wrong was that instead of just knocking down the slum dwellings, in their reforming zeal they destroyed many fine old houses around Glasgow Cross, the last of the half-timbered houses and the medieval houses around the Cathedral. While that was bad enough, under the guise of improving the Cathedral they mutilated it by demolishing its two medieval western towers. They also demolished buildings designed by the famous Adam brothers. Most inexcusable, however, was the greatest loss of all, the Old College in High Street, recognised as the finest group of seventeenth-century buildings in Scotland, which the University and the Council sacrificed to a railway company that demolished them.

Should we commend or condemn the Victorians for their redevelopment of the city? Possibly a bit of both as they did make the town a more pleasant and much healthier place to live, and if by removing the slums, which were the worst in the country, the picturesque was sacrificed, the means justified the end. Moreover, if they had not replaced the simple early eighteenth-century buildings extending west of Buchanan Street up to Blythswood Hill with exceptional office buildings designed by architects of outstanding merit, the city would not today be able to claim its title of 'the foremost Victorian city in the world'.

If the Victorians, whose buildings were, on the whole, worthy successors of the old, were not the worst vandals of Glasgow's historic buildings, who were? Our twentieth-century forebears, especially those of the 1960s and 70s, who blithely knocked down magnificent Victorian buildings and replaced them with concrete monstrosities that might have been economic and functional but added nothing to the street scene or the visual attractiveness of the city. In addition, the motorways, which began in the late 1960s to alleviate traffic congestion in the city, did more damage to it than had the Victorian railways.

The twentieth century had barely begun when Kelvingrove House, designed by Robert Adam, was demolished to make way for a section of the 1901 Exhibition. Eleven years later, the Adam brothers' Royal Infirmary was also demolished. There had been a public outcry, but public opinion rarely carried much weight in Glasgow when its leading citizens had made up their minds to do something. Actually, like its councils throughout the centuries, few Glaswegians bothered about buildings of historical or architectural merit. With a few exceptions, like the removal of the Cathedral towers, the Old College and some Adams' buildings, they were generally in favour of redevelopment.

Glasgow, unlike many other great industrial centres, suffered comparatively little damage from enemy action in the two World Wars. In the 1914–18 war bombs were dropped on Edinburgh but none on Glasgow. During the 1939–45 war Glasgow was bombed several times, and although George Square narrowly escaped destruction in a night raid in September 1940, it was in the last raid on Glasgow in March 1943 that the only real architectural loss was suffered – an Alexander 'Greek' Thomson church in Queen's Park. (The heavy and prolonged night raids in the spring of 1941 were mainly concentrated on Clydebank and Greenock.)

Despite requiring no post-war reconstruction, after the Second World War the city planners were determined to turn Glasgow into 'the most modern city in Europe'. They saw no merit in Victorian buildings, and if the plan put forward by Robert Bruce, the City Engineer, had been carried out, few if any of the city centre's historic buildings would still be around today. Because the city was emphatically against a loss of population, Bruce opposed the Clyde Valley Plan of 1946 proposing that new towns should be built to relieve Glasgow's housing problems. He wanted to demolish most of the city centre, including the City Chambers, and put up high-rise flats to house the population. Fortunately, Bruce's plan was not executed, and in the 1950s peripheral housing areas were created – Drumchapel, Easterhouse, Pollok and Castlemilk. His ring road plan, however, revised in the Glasgow Central Area Report and Highways Plan of 1965, had the greatest impact on the city centre by cutting it off from its immediate surroundings. Later, the east part of the ring road was altered so that St Andrew's Church and its environs were still within the city centre. The inner ring road cut through Anderston Cross, Charing Cross and St George's Cross, and obliterated Cowcaddens. Sharing the blame with Glasgow for the destruction was the Secretary of State for Scotland who approved it.

In 1964, when the Royal Institute of British Architects held its annual conference in Glasgow, architects from all over Britain, most of whom had never been in the city before and who were under the impression that it was a slum ready for demolition, were so astonished by the city's architecture that they said it had to be conserved at all costs. Chairman of the RIBA's planning committee, Lord Esher, could not believe what he saw and said it was a great city built of stone, far better than we could build today. 'We must preserve it,' he said.

To preserve it, however, was not the aim of the city fathers, and Frank Wordsall, in his book *The City That Disappeared*, makes mention of what happened when the newly formed conservationists The Victorian Group asked the Lord Provost to join an organised walk around the city centre to draw attention to the wealth of buildings there. The idea did not appeal to the

Lord Provost, who asked, 'Do they seriously suggest that the local authority should have to carry the financial burden of preserving all the city's Victorian buildings? I would not like the impression to get out that Glasgow was a Victorian city! Many old buildings will have to come down, and considering the state of them, whether Victorian or Edwardian, thank goodness for that.' With an attitude like that from its first citizen, is it any wonder so much of Glasgow's heritage vanished? Was it lack of education in matters architectural, no interest in the city's past, or just that it was believed that new was better? Whichever it was, Glasgow was in danger of losing buildings of architectural excellence unequalled in Britain.

A list of buildings of architectural or historic interest had been drawn up in the 1950s. However, as the greatest emphasis was on buildings dating from before 1700 and less significance was attached to a building the more recent it was, Glasgow was at a disadvantage – its buildings of interest were predominantly nineteenth and early twentieth century. Even the 1969 Act, which laid down that as an added precaution local authority consent had to be obtained before a listed building could be demolished, did not help Glasgow, as it was the local authority here that was doing the demolishing, often using the excuse that a particular building was dangerous and had to come down immediately. Other owners of old buildings were just as unscrupulous as the local authority, many deliberately allowing their properties to deteriorate in the hope that they would be allowed to demolish them.

In 1971 Glasgow appeared to have dropped its notorious hostility towards preservation and conservation, as it asked Lord Esher to make a general appraisal of the problems of building conservation in the city and to recommend what steps should be taken to set up and develop an effective policy for protecting and enhancing the city's good buildings and townscape. Among Lord Esher's many recommendations was the setting up of conservation areas such as Central, Kelvinside, Hillhead, Dowanhill, Pollokshields, Strathbungo and Dennistoun. (Today Glasgow has twenty conservation areas, ranging in character from the city centre and Victorian residential suburbs to the rural village of Carmunnock. These areas cover 1,423 hectares of the city and provide homes for 10 per cent of the population. The Central Conservation Area influences the commercial sector, both as a desirable working environment and as a visitor attraction.)

Lord Esher pointed out that conservation would cost money – from occupiers, the Corporation and central government – and would need consistent imaginative planning, but it would be worth it. 'A great many Victorian houses in their old settings and Victorian monuments in the city centre are built with more craftsmanship than we can hope to emulate or than the world is ever likely to see again.'

As the 1970s was the worst decade in the twentieth century for the demolition of irreplaceable architectural and historic buildings in Glasgow, the Corporation obviously took little notice of Lord Esher's recommendations. The exercise must just have been a ploy to keep conservationists quiet, as in 1972 the convener of the Highways Committee announced that he did not want the 'new Glasgow to be a museum piece for the delectation and delight of visiting professors of architecture'. (There was no danger of that as the over-ambitious plans of the Highways Committee were responsible for unparalleled destruction throughout the city.)

By the early 1980s the local authority's attitude to rehabilitation and conservation had begun to change, and many of the city centre's Victorian buildings were renovated and stone-cleaned. Demolition was not quite as extensive and sometimes buildings were retained although their interiors were gutted. Other times only the facades were retained and incorporated into new buildings.

Although nowadays the aim of Glasgow City Council is to protect, enhance and promote the city's rich and varied architectural heritage, if buildings of architectural or historic interest are to be retained, they need to be economically viable and functional. Owners are not interested in keeping them purely for their visual appeal, or for 'prestige' value, as the cost of maintaining them is incredibly high. Where maintenance has been ignored or where buildings have been vacated and become the target for vandalism, the Council can take statutory action against the owners to secure, repair or upgrade these buildings and return them to a productive use that may be different from their original purpose.

While it is clearly beneficial to find new uses for uneconomic obsolete buildings of architectural or historic interest, because of legislative controls restricting adaptation it is not always easy. Moreover, sometimes buildings have been so neglected that there is no option but to demolish them as they are either unsafe or reinstatement would be ruinously expensive. When that is the case, however, care should be taken to make sure redevelopment harmonises with existing buildings. Good-quality modern design can bring old and new together to create an attractive evolving urban landscape, and while Glasgow has various new buildings of which it can be proud, too many (particularly those of the 1960s and 70s) are shoddily built and of no architectural merit. Even if Glasgow had wanted to rebuild according to original designs, as did Germany, it could not have done so because, after the Second

World War, officials destroyed many of the old architectural drawings.

Some old buildings are made economically viable and functional by the addition of extra floors of modern design, which, despite being set back behind the cornice and parapet level to make them as unobtrusive as possible, often do not sit comfortably with the original architecture.

Scottish government ministers are responsible for identifying buildings of special architectural or historic interest throughout Scotland. Glasgow has around 1,800 buildings listed as being of special interest. They are graded A, B and C(S) according to their merits. Category A covers buildings of national and international importance, such as Glasgow School of Art, and accounts for 15.45 per cent of all listed buildings in Glasgow. Category B (69.65 per cent) takes in those of regional or local significance, and Category C(S) (14.90 per cent) contains buildings of more modest architectural or historic interest. The interiors and exteriors of category A, B and C (S) buildings are statutorily protected and are covered by a range of listed buildings controls – they may not be demolished or altered without prior listed-building consent from the local planning authority. (By the time of publication of *Lost Glasgow*, the number and categories of listed items in the city may have changed. Some buildings may have been demolished and others might have been reclassified as styles, attitudes and values change. Areas and buildings once seen as ordinary can, over time, be perceived in a different light, perhaps as well-preserved examples of a particular style. Historical evidence can also change the assessment of items.)

In conclusion, after many years of misguided planners undervaluing and destroying Glasgow's architectural heritage, today its planning authority, in tandem with heritage societies like Historic Scotland and the Scottish Civic Trust, does all in its power to ensure that the city remains the 'foremost Victorian city in the world'.

CAROL FOREMAN, 2002

CHAPTER 1
MEDIEVAL TOWN,
1175–1560

✳

Nothing is known of Glasgow's history for five centuries after the death in AD 603 of St Mungo, Glasgow's patron saint, who established a church and a community on the banks of the Molendinar Burn around AD 543. We can only begin to chart the development of the city from 1116, when King David I, then Prince of Cumbria, restored the see of Glasgow according to the canons of the Church of Rome and appointed his tutor, John Achaius, to the bishopric.

At David's command, one of Bishop Achaius' first duties was to detail all the lands and possessions that had once belonged to the church of St Mungo. This famous document, called 'The Inquest of David', listed the territorial possessions throughout the diocese, information that is invaluable as there is a dearth of records from that early period. Among the lands restored to the church were Ruglan (Rutherglen), Perdeyc (Partick) and Guven (Govan), all names that have survived until today. New lands were bestowed on the see when David became king. Under Achaius, the diocese was divided into two archdeaconries, Glasgow and Teviotdale, and various offices and prebends were established. A prebend is a share in the revenues of a cathedral or church allowed to a clergyman who officiates at stated times.

In 1124 Bishop Achaius began building a cathedral on the site of St Mungo's church, and after its consecration on 7 July 1136 the little cathedral town by the Molendinar began to play a part in the affairs of the kingdom.

Achaius was not only Bishop of Glasgow. He was Chancellor of Scotland and from the first had to fight the English claim that his bishopric owed obedience to the Archbishop of York. The fight was still going on in 1175 when Jocelin, Abbot of Melrose, was chosen to be fourth Bishop of Glasgow. No sooner was Jocelin elected, however, than he went to Rome and secured a papal order that the Scottish bishops should yield obedience to Rome alone. The diocese of Glasgow covered a large geographical area, with over 200 parishes from Luss in the north to Gretna in the south, and because of its importance was recognised by the Pope as a 'special daughter' of the Holy

George Henry's mural in the Banqueting Hall in the City Chambers representing King William the Lion granting the charter for the institution of Glasgow Fair.

See. The see was raised to an archbishopric in 1492 with jurisdiction over the bishoprics of Dunkeld, Dunblane, Galloway and Argyll.

As a reward for Jocelin's success in Rome, King William the Lion granted Glasgow a charter in 1175 making it a burgh of barony with the right to hold a weekly market on Thursdays. Being a burgh of barony meant that the city, and the church lands round it, belonged to the Bishop. He was the overlord of the whole area and, like any baron, had powers of life and death over his serfs and the right to collect taxes from the freemen living in the burgh. He also appointed the provost, bailies and sergeants of the town. In 1450, Glasgow became a burgh of regality, the Bishop representing the king's authority rather than, as before, ruling in his own right. It was not until 1611 that Glasgow became a royal burgh directly answerable only to Parliament and the king. In 1690, William and Mary granted the city 'the power and privilege to choose its own magistrates, provost, bailies and other officers'.

The presence of the Bishop, the clergymen connected with the Cathedral and their many servants, together with the additional wealth brought into the town from the revenues of the extensive diocese, resulted in the king granting the city the right in 1190 to hold a yearly fair. A fair was a valuable privilege, as without it the trade coveted by the Bishops could not have been attracted to their burghs. The fair was to be held for a week commencing 7 July. A charter of 1211 confirmed the fair, ordering the King's Peace to be kept during this time under a fine of 180 cows for manslaughter.

The fair established commerce in Glasgow, including trade with foreign countries, particularly France, with whom Glasgow had dealings from a very early period. A charter of 1363 says that among the articles on sale at the Glasgow Fair were French gloves and that Mary, Countess of Menteith, granted her kinsman Archibald, the son of Colin Campbell of Lochow, the lands of Kilmun on Cowal, the reddendo (service to be rendered) being the yearly payment of a pair of Paris gloves at Glasgow Fair.

As Bishop Achaius' cathedral had been destroyed by fire in 1192, Bishop Jocelin began rebuilding it, and in 1197 enough was ready for a rededication. Jocelin also built a tomb to St Mungo. Jocelin died on 17 March 1199 and was buried on the right-hand side of the Cathedral's choir. If it had not been for Jocelin's biography of St Mungo, Glasgow would have known nothing of its patron saint. It is also to Jocelin that Glasgow owes its burghal constitution, the institution of its markets and fair, and the foundation of its great church, which subsequent Bishops added to almost until the Reformation.

CATHEDRAL TOWERS

Additions to the Cathedral included the Consistory House and the Tower at the western end. The Consistory House, at the southwest, had probably been intended for a tower but instead of being carried up was finished with gables. In the ancient records, it is called the library house of the Cathedral and for 200 years the ecclesiastical courts were held in it. It was a picturesque building supported by buttresses and was lit on the south side by various windows, square-headed and pointed. The taller, square northwest Tower was 126 feet high, and on each side near the top were two windows with rounded arches. In the upper part of the Tower were grotesque sculptures. During its lifetime the Tower served as a prison, a court, a chapel and a burial place. Although it is not known exactly when the Consistory House and Tower were built, the mid-thirteenth century is thought to be correct.

Apart from their antiquity, both buildings were valuable in adding to the beauty of the Cathedral, and the Tower, although not in keeping with other parts of the building, was essential to the proper balance of the structure. Yet, incredibly, in the 1840s the Consistory House and the Tower, both in a perfect state of preservation, were pulled down. At the time, the *Glasgow Herald* noted that a man was seen stirring the burning rubbish – the priceless post-Reformation records of the Cathedral.

One excuse for the vandalism was that two finer towers, which would

View of Glasgow Cathedral with the Consistory House and Tower intact.

improve the Cathedral, would replace the Consistory House and the Tower. Other excuses were that the Tower was an eyesore out of keeping with the Cathedral's magnificence and that the Consistory House and the Tower were later in date than the nave and therefore not part of the original church design. When the Tower was demolished, however, it was found that the aisle window against which it had been built had never been glazed, proving that the Tower was added after the nave had been started but before it was finished. If the Tower did not form part of the original design of the Cathedral, therefore, its erection must have been decided on before the nave was completed. The Victorian architect John Honeyman believed the Tower to be coeval with the nave and fellow architect R. W. Billings thought the west doorway of the nave and the lower stage of the Tower were the oldest portions of the Cathedral.

While Glasgow's Victorian city fathers considered the Consistory House and Tower to be unimportant architecturally, old council minutes prove that their predecessors had regarded them as part of the ancient structure, thus equally deserving preservation with the other parts of the Cathedral.

When it was decided to demolish the Consistory House and Tower there was a public outcry, but despite important people, many of them architects, remonstrating with the council the Consistory House was demolished in 1846 and the Tower in 1848. When the Tower was removed, a large tombstone was

Drawing of the west elevation of Glasgow Cathedral showing the Consistory House and Tower.

found in the centre of the floor of the chapel with an armorial bearing on a corner, thought to have been the arms of the fourteenth-century Cardinal Walter Wardlaw. Before anyone could be found to properly decipher the arms, however, the stone was broken up and built into the north buttress of the west side of the Cathedral. The removal of the Tower was described as an act of barbarism.

Although Glasgow has never been kind to its old buildings, the removal of the Consistory House and the Tower was the worst desecration of a building in the city and the mutilated Cathedral remains to this day a monument to ignorance.

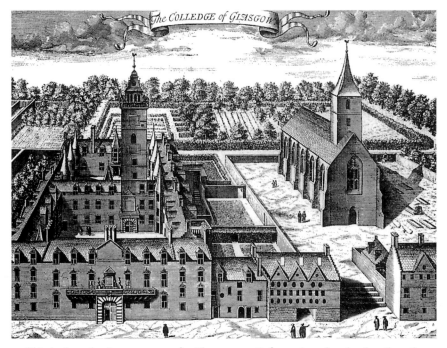

This is the only picture extant of a Glasgow pre-Reformation church other than the Cathedral. It is from Captain John Abraham Slezer's Theatrum Scotiae, *published in London in 1693. The volume contained fifty-seven large 'prospects' of Scotland, three being of Glasgow – the Merchants' Hill (the Necropolis), the south river-front, and a bird's-eye view of the College and Blackfriars Church. The view was taken shortly before lightning destroyed the church.*

BLACKFRIARS CHURCH

The Cathedral was not the only church in medieval Glasgow. There was also the church of the Black Friars. On the east side of the thoroughfare that became High Street Pope Gregory had founded a monastery in 1240 for the Dominicans, or Black Friars, whose church was built before 1246 – possibly in the preceding century. When King Edward I of England was in Glasgow in 1301, he lodged with the Black Friars, their establishment being the only place in the town capable of receiving the royal retinue. Like other Dominican buildings, it would have been highly furnished. The church, which had a steeple similar to that of the Cathedral, was described by Glasgow's first historian, M'ure, as 'the ancientest building of Gothic kind of work that could be seen in the whole kingdom'.

After the Reformation, the Crown bestowed Blackfriars Church upon

Front view of Old College Church, 1848.

Glasgow University, at that time still in the same part of town. In 1670 light-ning struck the church, splitting the steeple from top to bottom and setting it on fire. The church was never restored and lay in ruins for years until a new church of a very different style was erected in its place in 1701. This was the Old College Church, which was demolished in the 1880s when the University moved to Gilmorehill.

BISHOP'S CASTLE

Next in importance to Glasgow Cathedral was the Bishop's Castle (roughly where the Royal Infirmary now stands), the residence and administrative headquarters of the Bishop, who had secular and spiritual responsibility for the burgh.

There are no records to show when the Castle of Glasgow, for such it was, was built. The first mention of it is in 1258 in the Chartulary of Glasgow (Chartulary – the city register), which refers to Bishop William de Bondington and states: 'His palace is without the Castle of Glasgow'. The name Castle appears again in 1268 and 1290 when it is said to have a garden.

Painting by Thomas Hearne, c. 1782, of the Bishop's Castle with Bishop Cameron's Tower in the foreground. In the background is Glasgow Cathedral. The single-storey building across from the Tower was known as Darnley's Cottage as it was built on the site of the Erskine Manse where Lord Darnley was alleged to have lodged in January 1567 when he was sick with smallpox and where his wife, Mary Queen of Scots, visited him.

Although the appearance and extent of the original Castle are uncertain, it is known that around 1438 Bishop Cameron added a great tower and that about 1510 Archbishop Beaton fortified it with a 15-foot-high wall with a bastion, ditch and tower. Archbishop Dunbar built the last addition around 1530, a towered gatehouse.

The Castle was both palace and stronghold, and in 1300 an English garrison held it until Wallace's victory of the Bell o' the Brae (the steep part of High Street that led to the Cathedral). When John Mure of Caldwell and others stormed and plundered the Castle in 1515, Archbishop Beaton began an action against Mure for 'Wrangwis spoliation' and detailed the goods stolen. Mure had to make restitution. It was after this raid that Archbishop Beaton built the 15-foot high wall.

When the Earl of Lennox's men garrisoned the Castle in 1544, the Earl of Arran, who acted as regent during the minority of Mary Queen of Scots, besieged it for ten days. The garrison surrendered under a promise of mercy that was not honoured. Arran hanged all but a few of the twenty-four defenders. In 1560, while Mary of Guise was regent, her French soldiers garrisoned the Castle. When the Protestant lords, under Arran, besieged it, the Frenchmen surrendered. Some of the Frenchmen died when gunpowder exploded within the Castle.

The Castle suffered badly during the Reformation but was used as a fortress and a council chamber until around 1611, when the Protestant Archbishop Spottiswood partially restored the building and lived in it, as did his successors, Law and Lindsay.

Episcopacy was abolished by the General Assembly held in Glasgow in 1638, and for twenty-three years Glasgow had no archbishops. The Restoration of Charles II in 1660 brought with it the re-establishment of episcopacy, and it was not until the 'Glorious' Revolution in 1688, which brought William and Mary to the throne in place of James II, that it was finally abolished in Scotland. From then, the former Bishop's Palace began to decay, with citizens taking stones from it for building purposes. In 1715, it was used as a prison, 353 Jacobite prisoners being held in it, guarded by 100 soldiers and fed at the city's expense.

Although historians tell us that the Saracen's Head Inn in Gallowgate was built from stones taken from the crumbling walls of the Bishop's Castle, the truth is that in 1754 the council decided to demolish the old East Port, which formed an obstruction in the Gallowgate, the main eastern thoroughfare. It also decided to sell the site of Little St Mungo's Kirk, adjacent to the East Port. The council then gave the purchaser of the site permission to use the stones from the East Port for building purposes, not those from the Bishop's Castle. The purchaser built the Saracen's Head Inn on the site, and there is no proof that any stones from the Bishop's Castle were used in its erection.

Even in the eighteenth century, Glasgow's leaders had little respect for the city's ancient buildings, and to allow the Bishop's Castle to go to wrack and ruin was an unparalleled act of vandalism equalled only by the removal of the two Cathedral Towers. The ruins of the Castle were cleared away in 1792 to make way for Robert Adam's Royal Infirmary.

There are two reminders of the Castle. The first are two carved stones in the Cathedral with a plaque saying: 'These stones from a doorway of the former Bishop's Castle were placed here in 1965. Below the arms of James V,

Ruins of the Bishop's Castle as they stood in 1789.

King of Scots, are those of Gavin Dunbar, Archbishop of Glasgow 1524–47 and of James Houston, sub dean.' The second is a memorial stone in Cathedral Square, presented to the city by the Lord Dean of Guild, Francis Henderson, to mark the site.

FORMATION OF THE TOWN

Medieval Glasgow consisted of two centres, the ecclesiastical upper town on its hill and the lay lower town near the river where the fishing and trades people lived. The town plan is not difficult to construct. It took the form of a cross twice repeated.

There was Glasgow Cathedral on high ground on the west bank of the Molendinar, with the Bishop's Castle nearby. South from the Cathedral ran the straggling track that became High Street, which was crossed just below the Cathedral by Rottenrow from the west and Drygate from the east. The cross formed the first centre of Glasgow, and the space at its intersection was called the Quadrivium, or Wyndhead.

The second centre was where the north-south line of the High Street track and its continuation, Walcargate (Saltmarket), was crossed by St Thenew's Gate (Trongate) on the west and the Gallowgate on the east. At the end of the twelfth century, when the first bridge, the 'brig of tre', was built across the River Clyde at the foot of Fishergate (Stockwell Street), the track at the foot of Walcargate, which swung sharply round to the right to meet the bridge head, became known as Bridgegate, 'the way to the bridge'. The first reference to the bridge dates from 1285 when it is mentioned in documents recording the sale of a 'burgage' (tenure of property) in Fishergate.

By the 1300s, therefore, when the population was 1,500, Glasgow had eight main thoroughfares – the track that became High Street, Rottenrow, Drygate, St Thenew's Gate, Gallowgate, Bridgegate, Fishergate and Walcargate.

Fishergate got its name from a row of huts mentioned in a charter of 1285 as belonging to the salmon fishers. Because of this, the area became known as *viscus piscatorum*, the Fishergate. It became Stockwell Street when a well that was worked with a wooden stock was erected at its Trongate end. Walcargate got its name because it was inhabited chiefly by fullers, or walkers as they were known in Scotland. It became Saltmarket around the middle of the sixteenth century when the salt market was there. St Thenew's Gate was the way to the Chapel of St Thenew, near to today's St Enoch Square, Enoch being a corruption of Thenew. The erection around 1500 in St Thenew's Gate of a 'tron', a public weighing machine used to assess duty on all marketable produce, led to the street being called Trongate.

Of these thoroughfares, Drygate (pre-1100) was the oldest, followed by Rottenrow. Although an ancient track, High Street appears to have had no name and in a conveyance of 1418 property there is referred to as being in the street that extends from the Cathedral to the market cross. This was the first direct reference to Glasgow Cross, then at the intersection of Rottenrow and Drygate. A document of 1433 calls High Street 'the gat at strekis fra the mercat cors tyll the Hie Kirk of Glasgow'. In fact, High Street, which became the backbone of the town, was of little account until the University was located there. It was just a means of getting from the upper town to the lower town.

The pace of economic development in Glasgow was slow, and in 1367 the city was ranked as only twenty-first out of thirty-four burghs represented in the league table of monies paid as taxes to the crown. In fact, in 1357 Glasgow was so inconsequential as not to be admitted to the number of cautionary towns assigned to King Edward III of England for the payment of the ransom of King David II of Scotland. At the time the city was mainly confined to the ridge that extends from the Cathedral, the houses encroaching very little on the ground on each side.

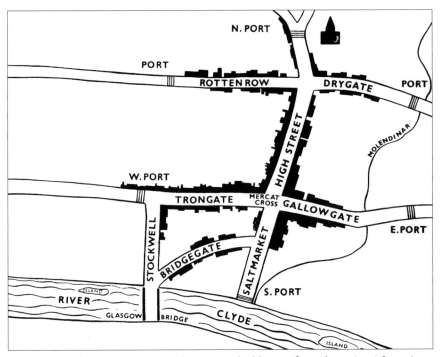

A concept of medieval Glasgow, showing its double cruciform shape, its eight main streets, the Molendinar Burn, Glasgow Bridge and the ports.

Glasgow was never a walled city, but dykes that enclosed the gardens of the small houses surrounded it, and where each road met the open country, a port closed it. These ports ('gates' from French) sealed the ends of streets and consisted of a large stone archway and two great wooden gates that could be closed at night or during the day if there were danger. In times of plague the ports were guarded by day and locked at night, and any burgess who failed to take his turn on guard duty armed with a halberd was fined. At those times travellers were not allowed to enter the city unless they could prove they had come from uninfected areas. Plague raged in medieval Glasgow in 1350, 1380 and 1381.

In 1175 there were three ports barring the traveller's way into the city, the East Port in the Gallowgate, the West Port in St Thenew's Gate and the South Port at the foot of Walcargate . By 1325 two more ports had been added, the Brig Port on the east of the north side of the bridge and the Water Port on the west side. Later came others like the Drygate Port, the Stable Green Port near the wall surrounding the Castle and the Castle Yett Port opposite the Castle.

For centuries the popular view was that the upper town grew to meet the lower town. Less popular was the view that the lower town expanded up towards the Cathedral. Andrew Gibb in his book, *Glasgow, The Making of a City*, believes the latter view to be correct. This, he says, is based on re-examination of datable evidence for building activity in relation to the physical characteristics of the site and, especially, the indications of colonisation of a broad fringe belt lying between the market and the Cathedral.

The truth about whether the city developed southwards or northwards has been lost in the mists of time, but it does seem likely that the lower town predated the creation of the burgh in 1176, as for this to happen there must have been some existing form of mercantile activity. In addition, that a bridge had been built over the River Clyde at the end of the twelfth century suggests growing trade in the lower town.

Glasgow's foreign trade began in the lower town, William Elphinstone being credited with pioneering it. Around 1450 he began a business of curing salmon and herrings, which he exported to France. In return, he brought back wine, salt, brandy and continental luxuries – fine cloth, lace, silk and velvets.

OLD GLASGOW BRIDGE

By the middle of the fourteenth century, trade in the lower town had expanded, and in 1350 Bishop Rae had the old wooden bridge pulled down and, at his own expense, had it replaced by a stone twelve-foot-wide eight-arched bridge, called Glasgow Bridge, which stood for about 500 years. Lady Lochow is said to have helped the Bishop by paying for one arch. (Some debate the bridge being ascribed to Bishop Rae and whether Lady Lochow was involved, but the story has become too deeply embedded in the history of Glasgow to discredit.) The bridge, then the western boundary of Glasgow, was looked upon as a wonderful piece of work and was mentioned as *Magnum Pons trans Cludan* – the 'great bridge over the Clyde'.

After 300 years of traffic, it was no wonder that an order was passed in 1658 to prevent wheeled carts from crossing the bridge – the wheels had to be taken off and the carts 'harled' across by the horse. So unsafe was the bridge believed to be that often carters and horsemen crossed the river at the shallow ford near the bridge.

Some people did not use the bridge for another reason – to avoid the council officers who collected bridge dues and market tolls. From every sack of grain, flour and meal, the officers would take a ladleful and a proportion (generally one out of each basket) from such produce as eggs, potatoes, fish

This etching by James Brown, c. 1776, shows the north end of the medieval Glasgow Bridge, which had a steep ascent to its centre and was so narrow that 'wheelbarrows trembled when they met'. The illustration shows coaches crossing the bridge and carts crossing by the ford above the bridge. It also shows that there was a ford below the bridge. A council minute of 24 November 1767 confirms that there were two fords, as it mentions 'the foords above and below the bridge of Glasgow'. The 'Brig Port' is shown at the north end of the bridge.

and cheese. These were called 'ladle dues', and as the money obtained from them was spent on keeping the streets in good order the toll was sometimes called 'gait dichting', or street cleansing. Coins were scarce so this was the easiest way to collect the bridge tax.

In 1671 the southernmost arch of the bridge fell down. This was on 7 July, during Glasgow Fair, and although great crowds had used the bridge that day, luckily no lives were lost. By 1765 the bridge had deteriorated so much that the magistrates tried to close it completely to carts. This suggestion was resisted by the inhabitants of Rutherglen and led in 1776 to the bridge being widened by ten feet on the eastern side and the two north arches being built up to prevent danger in times of spates on the river. In 1821 the bridge was overhauled to a design by Thomas Telford, who added footpaths suspended from iron framings. In 1847, however, owing to the great increase in traffic, Old Glasgow Bridge, the oak foundations of which were still solid after 500 years, was removed and replaced by the present Victoria Bridge.

PREBENDARY MANSES

While the lower town consisted of dwellings for the trades people and the fishing community, ecclesiastical holdings dominated the upper town – the Cathedral, the Bishop's Castle, charitable establishments and the manses of the prebendaries, or rectors, who served the Cathedral as canons. These clergymen made up the Cathedral chapter, elected the bishop and helped with the administration of the diocese. They were supported financially by their prebend, or living, usually a parish elsewhere in the diocese from which they obtained rent and taxes. As the clergymen were required to live near the Cathedral during their term of service, they were ordered to build manses in the city.

It could be said that the start of these manses was when Bishop Jocelin granted a Glasgow house to his old abbey in 1195, the house being described as the first building to be erected in the burgh. However, it was Bishop John de Cheyan, by a statute of 1266, who first ordered the manses to be built. By 1401 there were twenty-three, and a further order issued around 1430 by Bishop Cameron increased the number to thirty-two. Most of the manses, which had gardens at the back, were in Drygate, Rottenrow and on the west of the Cathedral (now Castle Street). Grouped near the Cathedral and the Bishop's Palace, the stone-built manses gave the upper part of town a character distinct from that of the lower town where the houses of the artisans were timber framed and less well built.

As well as the manses, there were noblemen's town houses, and just to the north of the Cathedral, Vicars' Alley joined manses for thirty-two or so vicars, divided by a wide central courtyard into two facing terraces. (In the absence of the prebendaries, their duties were performed, in the Cathedral or parish church, by vicars.)

THE MANSE OF LUSS (AULD PEDAGOGY)
*

The Rector of Luss did not build his manse, which was situated on the south side of Rottenrow. Its history goes back much further than his occupancy. First mentioned in a deed of 1283, it was supposed to have been used as a chapterhouse of the Cathedral before the Papal foundation of the university, which it also housed in its infancy.

Bishop Turnbull had persuaded James II to apply to Pope Nicholas V to found a university in Glasgow, 'a notable place enjoying a salubrious atmos-

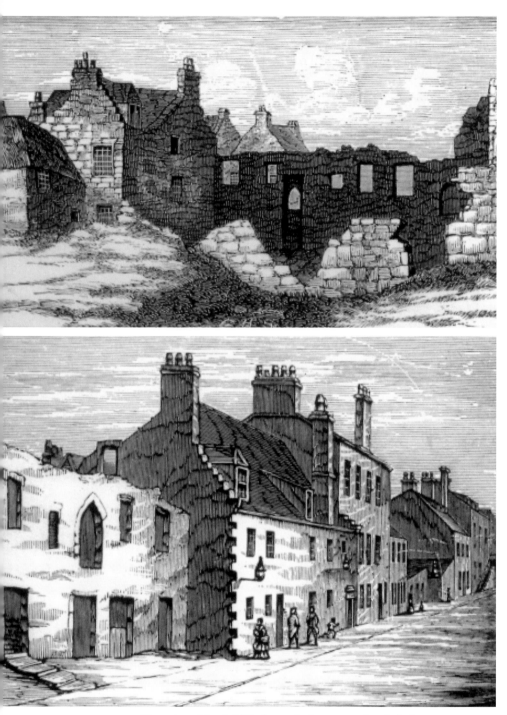

The ruins of the Auld Pedagogy in Rottenrow shortly before
they were removed about 1860.

phere and abundance of all the necessaries of life'. Nicholas agreed and in January 1451 issued a bull for the setting up of a 'Stadium Generale', or University, in Glasgow, modelled on the University of Bologna in which he had taught.

At first classes were held in the chapterhouse of the Cathedral but were then transferred to the old house on the south side of Rottenrow which became known as the 'Auld Pedagogy'. Apart from classrooms, the building provided living quarters for the students and a common hall.

When the University moved out of the Auld Pedagogy around 1459, the building went through many changes, becoming, for example, the Manse of Luss and later a Presbyterian manse. For a long time, however, it was in an appalling state, with grass growing inside the ruined walls and not as much as a rafter or piece of wood remaining. The walls were three feet thick, and there were the remains of a circular arched door, two fireplaces and a large window of ecclesiastical design. What was left of one of the oldest medieval buildings in the city was removed about 1860 and the infamous Lock Hospital for 'dangerous women' with sexually transmitted diseases was built on the site. The hospital was demolished in 1955.

THE DOUGLAS MANSE
*

The Douglas Manse in Drygate had a connection with prison life. In 1637 it became the town's first Bridewell, or Correction House, not a jail like the Tolbooth but an industrial reformatory. It was also used as a place for whipping lawbreakers. Built in 1500, the building had previously been the house of the Rector of Douglas and the Earl of Eglinton. During the Earl's occupation, James VI was his guest in 1617 when the king last visited Glasgow. The building ceased to be the Bridewell in 1788 and was demolished about 1822. Duke Street Prison was later erected close by where the Bridewell had stood. When the prison was demolished in 1960 and a housing scheme was built on the site, Drygate practically vanished.

THE DUKE'S LODGINGS (THE PEEBLES MANSE)
*

The Duke's Lodgings, a building on the south side of Drygate, was created out of the Rector of Peebles' Manse (1446) and the tenement adjoining it, which had belonged to the Stewarts of Minto, an important family in

The only view of the Manse of Douglas that exists is an engraving of 1762 of the back of the building. It is interesting as it shows the gardens on the south side of Drygate as they were at the Reformation.

Glasgow, some members having been provosts. After the Reformation, Sir Matthew Stewart bought the Peebles Manse and rebuilt the tenement to correspond to it in height and size.

The Montrose family bought the property, and when James, the first duke, transformed it into an arcaded courtyard mansion with gardens and a gazebo it was nicknamed the Duke's Lodgings. The building had a distinguished visitor in July 1651 when Oliver Cromwell and his Ironsides camped around it, all very civilly but making free use of garden vegetables and standing grain.

After a couple of changes of ownership, the property was divided into separate homes. The kitchen fireplace was so large it had been made into a separate room, and, according to the editor of *Swan's Views*, in 1829 a family of four lived in it. Having bought the building in 1849, the Prison Board demolished it in 1851 to make way for an extension to Duke Street Prison.

It would be a mistake to believe that life for the clergy who lived in the manses was spartan. Documentation indicates otherwise. A full inventory of the Stobo Manse made in 1542 shows that the priest had a wardrobe of costly clothing and a great deal of expensive furniture. He also had Flemish tapestries, armour and hunting gear, which would not have been out of place in a noble household. The Stobo Manse was said to have been the old Mint where coins were struck. The Mint House was built around 1392.

The Duke's Lodgings depicted by William Simpson in the 1840s, probably the grandest nobleman's house in old Glasgow.

William Simpson's painting of the south side of Drygate with Rottenrow in the distance shows what the street looked like in 1843 when it had a mixture of buildings belonging to different centuries. The thatched building, the Manse of Eaglesham, was built around 1440. Next to it the tall, narrow Manse of Stobo, which looked more like a tower than a dwelling house, was thought to be fourteenth century. Beside the Stobo Manse is a picturesque seventeenth-century tenement topped by two large half-timbered gables. From left to right: Eaglesham Manse, Stobo Manse and the seventeenth-century gabled building. All these buildings and the south side of Drygate disappeared into the grounds of Duke Street Prison as it was periodically expanded.

St Nicholas Hospital

*

As the city increased in population and importance, caring for the poor and less fortunate was seen as a principal role of the bishop, and charitable establishments were founded, such as St Nicholas Hospital. The Hospital, close to the Bishop's Castle, was founded and endowed by Bishop Andrew Muirhead in 1471 to house twelve poor old men. The Hospital buildings comprised the old men's house, a cottage for the female servants, a hall and a chapel. Adjoining the buildings on the north side was the manse for the priest in charge of the Hospital. The manse was also the house of the prebendary of

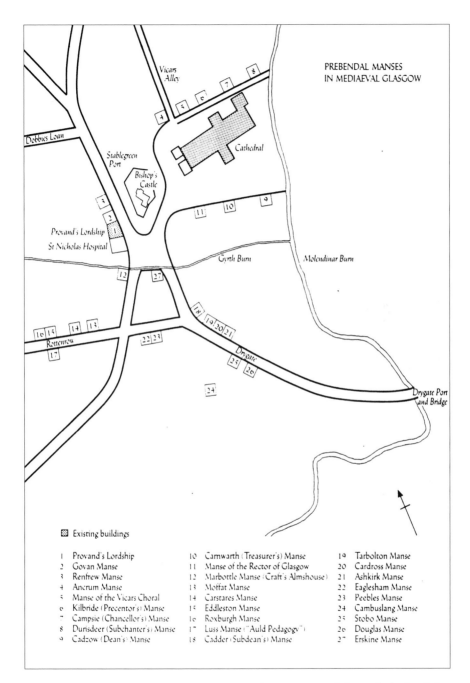

PREBENDAL MANSES
IN MEDIAEVAL GLASGOW

Vicars Alley

Dobbies Loan

Stablegreen Port

Bishop's Castle

Cathedral

Provand's Lordship

St Nicholas Hospital

Gyrth Burn

Molendinar Burn

Rottenrow

Drygate

Drygate Port and Bridge

▨ Existing buildings

1	Provand's Lordship	10	Carnwarth (Treasurer's) Manse	19	Tarbolton Manse
2	Govan Manse	11	Manse of the Rector of Glasgow	20	Cardross Manse
3	Renfrew Manse	12	Marbottle Manse (Craft's Almshouse)	21	Ashkirk Manse
4	Ancrum Manse	13	Moffat Manse	22	Eaglesham Manse
5	Manse of the Vicars Choral	14	Carstares Manse	23	Peebles Manse
6	Kilbride (Precentor's) Manse	15	Eddleston Manse	24	Cambuslang Manse
7	Campsie (Chancellor's) Manse	16	Roxburgh Manse	25	Stobo Manse
8	Durisdeer (Subchanter's) Manse	17	Luss Manse ("Auld Pedagogy")	26	Douglas Manse
9	Cadzow (Dean's) Manse	18	Cadder (Subdean's) Manse	27	Erskine Manse

A hypothetical map showing the arrangement of manses around the Cathedral and the Bishop's Castle. Only twenty-seven are accounted for. As many manses changed hands from one pebendary to another, the names changed accordingly. There were also times when the manses were rented to people unconnected with the church.

*The chapel of St Nicholas with buttresses and steeple about 1780. To the left are the
ruins of the hall and to the right part of the ruined tower of the Bishop's Palace.*

Barlanark, also known as Provan, the most important man in the diocese next
to the Bishop. Now known as Provand's Lordship, the building, much
altered, is, along with the Cathedral, all that remains of medieval Glasgow.

The old men's house, cottage and hall were removed in 1798, but the
chapel, which stood back from the building line, remained until 1808 when it
was taken down despite the council's promise to preserve it as it was a rear
building and would not affect the building line. The Barony Church is built
on the site of St Nicholas Hospital.

THE TRADES' ALMSHOUSE
(MOREBATTLE MANSE)

*

Another charitable institution was that of the Trades House, which consisted
of fourteen Incorporations of Glasgow's trades people and set up an
almshouse in 1605 in the Morebattle Manse just south of St Nicholas

The Trades' Almshouse, the old Manse of Morebattle, the name deriving from the home of the Archdeacon of Teviotdale. The building was in good repair when it was taken down in 1865.

Hospital. Built around 1440 as the Glasgow residence of the Archdeacon of Teviotdale, the building was adapted by the Incorporations to house at first five and then thirteen poor Freemen of the Trades' rank who were clothed in an ample coat, waistcoat and knee-breeks of blue serge.

Although small, the Morebattle Manse was the most tasteful of all the manses. It had a turret staircase at the back giving access to the upper rooms. When adapted by the Trades House, the upper rooms were divided by wooden partitions and later the stone wall in the upstairs portion was cut to form the Trades Hall, where, after the almshouse period, members of the crafts held their meetings until 1792 when they moved into a new building in Glassford Street designed by Robert Adam.

When funerals passed on the way to the Cathedral, an almshouse resident would toll a small bell in the turret. In appreciation the mourners would deposit a small donation in a box placed in an almshouse window above which were the words cut in stone: 'Give to the puir and thou sal have treasur in Heavin – Matt xix chap.'

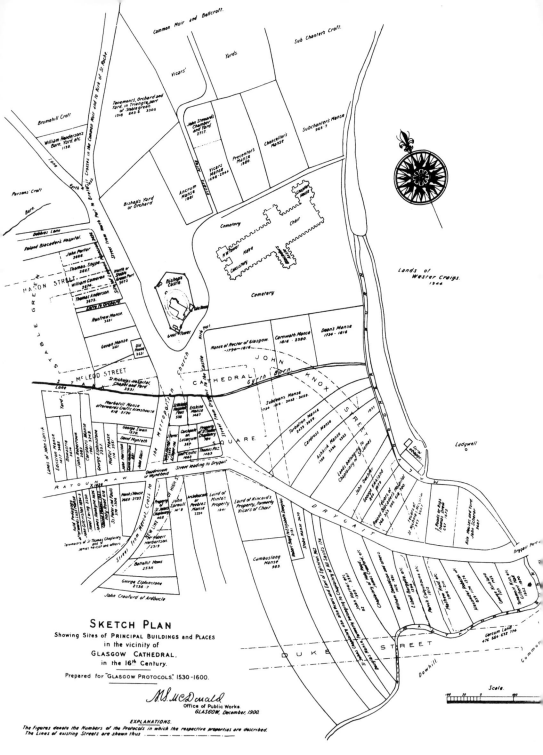

*Conjectural plan prepared for Robert Renwick's History of Glasgow in 1921,
showing sites of principal buildings and places in the vicinity of
Glasgow Cathedral in the sixteenth century.*

Cottages in High Street from a watercolour by Andrew Donaldson, c. 1817.
Although from an artist's point of view old buildings like the cottages were picturesque,
in reality the ramshackle inflammable buildings were vermin-ridden breeding
grounds for disease and horrendous to live in.

THE HIGH STREET

Just before the Reformation, High Street began to be filled in with a jumble of buildings like those illustrated. Alongside simple one-storey cottages of stone and turf covered with thatch were two-storey wooden-fronted buildings. The top storey projected further over the street than the one below it.

PORTERFIELD HOUSE
*

Not all the new buildings in High Street were humble dwellings. Porterfield House, standing directly opposite Blackfriars Church, was a mansion. Built around 1550, the house was acquired by John Porterfield in 1553 from the chaplain to the altar of the Blessed Virgin Mary, in the parish of Houston, diocese of Glasgow.

The stone-built house was originally plain with a round projecting staircase at the back. The gabled wing, broad flight of steps, larger windows and

Old houses in the 'Bell o' the Brae', the name given to the steep part of High Street that led to the Cathedral. During the eighteenth and nineteenth centuries, the gradient of the Bell o' the Brae was lowered.

capped dormers were alterations made by George Porterfield, Provost of Glasgow from 1645 to 1649 and again in 1651. Like the manses, the walls of Porterfield House were three feet thick and the basement was strongly arched, leading to the belief that the main fabric may have been built in the fifteenth century. The house sat in its own garden and orchard, and the site had been chosen before there was any regular west building line in High Street at that part.

In 1870, when Ingram Street was extended to High Street, Porterfield House was demolished and another part of old Glasgow was lost. There is a story, however, that when the house was being knocked down a man walking up High Street had a word with the contractor overseeing the demolition and

*Watercolour of Porterfield House by William Simpson. Thomas Lugton, in his
The Old Ludgings of Glasgow, said that the flight of steps and dormer windows of
Porterfield House added by George Porterfield were identical in design to those made
at Provanhall by the Dean of Guild in 1668 and may have been the work of the same
mason, the only difference being that Provanhall, being a smaller house, had the size
of the steps and dormers proportionately smaller. Parts of Provanhall are
thought to be as old as Provand's Lordship (1471).*

bought from him one of the house's inner doors. The door became the dining-room door of the man's west-end house.

By the middle of the sixteenth century, when the population had reached 4,500, the economic affairs of the city had moved from the upper town to the area around Glasgow Cross, which by then was at the intersection of Gallowgate and Trongate. High Street had been filled with buildings, as had Saltmarket and Bridgegate. Gallowgate had developed to the Dovehill and Trongate had extended to the collegiate church dedicated to the Blessed Virgin Mary (now the Tron Church), built about 1540 and burned down accidentally by the Hell Fire Club in 1793. Fortunately, the steeple was saved. To the eight medieval thoroughfares had been added Bun's Wynd, the Old Vennel and the Back Cow Loan (today's Ingram Street). That, then, was the extent of Glasgow on the eve of the Reformation.

CHAPTER 2
THE REFORMATION
TO THE ACT OF UNION
1560–1707

✳

REFORMATION

When the Reformation came, the authority of the Pope was abolished in Scotland and it was made penal to say mass. Although Glasgow's Archbishop, James Beaton, tried to make a stand against the reformers in July 1560, a month before the Scottish Parliament recognised the reformed faith as the established religion of the land, he fled to France never to return. With him he took the records and treasures of the see. The archives, which included the original burgh charter, a protocol book, a rental and two cartularies, one, the Red Book of Glasgow (the burgh records dating from the reign of Robert III), were deposited in the Scots College in Paris, where they remained until the outbreak of the French Revolution. They were then sent for safety to St Omer. Although most of them were never recovered, the Scottish Catholic Archives are in possession of the protocol book, the rental and one of the two cartularies. The other, the Red Book, is in the Scottish Record Office. The loss of the invaluable archives is the main reason for the scanty knowledge of Glasgow's pre-Reformation history.

Even though abbeys, monasteries and churches were pillaged and burned during the Reformation, Glasgow Cathedral escaped the destructive violence of the reformers and, except for the lead being stripped from its roof, the fabric of the building was largely undamaged. This, legend tells us, was thanks to members of the trades guilds who are reputed to have saved it from demolishment in 1579 by taking up arms and declaring to the workmen about to do the deed that 'he who would cast down the first stone shall be buried under it'. Only when the magistrates gave the order to down tools did they move. The story has never been authenticated. It is often written that Glasgow Cathedral and Kirkwall Cathedral are the only Scottish medieval cathedrals to have survived the Reformation. This is not true. St Magnus on Orkney was built when the islands were not yet part of Scotland so Glasgow is the only medieval cathedral in Scotland to have survived the Reformation.

Although the Cathedral was left standing, all the images and altars in the choir and nave (each of the richly decorated altars having a separate endowment) were destroyed on instructions from the Protestant Lords of the Congregation. Also destroyed was all the painted glass, and some of the beautiful choir windows were roughly built up with stone to save the expense of putting more glass in them. The nave also fell into disrepair.

Very little was done to prevent the fabric of the church from falling into ruin until 1637 when the magistrates were forced to put it into better order. With so many distinguished visitors and strangers coming to Glasgow to attend the General Assembly in 1638, they were anxious to make both the church and the city look respectable. While the repairs prevented the fabric from collapsing, the church continued in a sadly neglected state until the restoration of the nineteenth century, marred by the act of vandalism (removal of the two Towers) described in the previous chapter.

An immediate result of the Reformation was the decay of the medieval ecclesiastical city. The prebendary manses inhabited largely by clergy were left tenantless. The Bishop's Castle still stood next to the Cathedral but unoccupied by a bishop. The centre of Glasgow's life moved south to the Cross, situated where the four streets of the medieval lower town converged.

GROWTH OF TRADE

Although seventeenth-century Glasgow was essentially a pleasant university town, it was then that the foundations of its future prosperity through trading were laid. By the mid-century, it was trading with France, Ireland, Norway, the Mediterranean countries and the Caribbean. Cloth factories, the only soap work in Scotland, sugar refineries and a candle industry were set up. Curing of herrings was a profitable business and merchants had started trading in tobacco. They sent finished goods to Virginia and Maryland and received tobacco leaf in return.

In 1662 a small quay was built on the River Clyde at the Broomielaw, and in 1668 a new port was built downriver on the Firth of Clyde at Newark, which was renamed Port Glasgow. Over the years, attempts were made to deepen the Clyde to allow larger ships to reach the heart of the city. No real progress was made, however, until 1768 when Chester engineer John

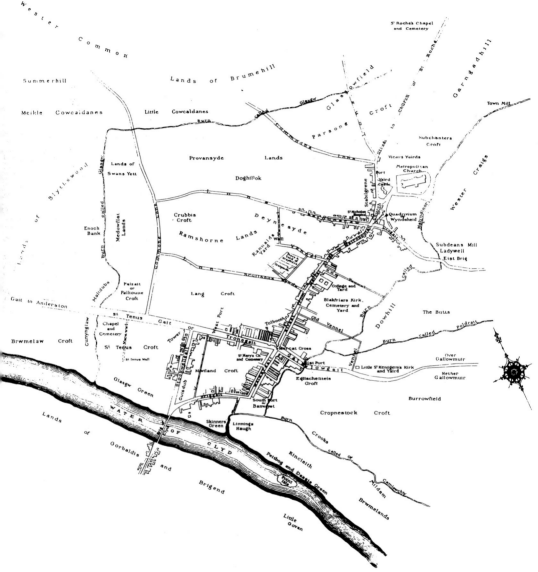

Conceptual plan of the City of Glasgow about 1560 prepared by the Office of Public Works for Robert Renwick's History of Glasgow, 1921. Note that the Cathedral is called the Metropolitan Church and High Street is the street from Mercat Cross to the Metropolitan Church. The only bridge across the river was the Brig of Clyd. Other names are still recognisable.

Old houses in Drygate, c. 1650.

Golborne came up with an effective plan – to throw the current into the centre of the river by means of jetties and help the natural scour of the water further by dredging the channel. In 1775 the Clyde was navigable to vessels drawing six feet of water, which were able for the first time to come up to the Broomielaw at high tide.

TOWNSCAPE AND BUILDINGS

While between 1560 and 1707 the population of Glasgow had risen from 4,500 to around 12,000, the town had spread very little from its medieval boundaries. To the original eight streets only one had been added – Candleriggs, which opened in 1668. The people were not migratory and, instead of forming new streets in the spacious fields, preferred to build within wynds (lanes) running off existing thoroughfares. Before 1707, the wynds were Bun's, Grammar School, Blackfriars, Bell's, the Old Vennel and the New Vennel, all of which were off High Street. In the lower town were Gibson's Wynd,

Upper Town in the 1670s, from J. Slezer's Theatrum Scotiae. *The view is to the northeast of the city. The Cathedral and Bishop's Castle are to the right, and in the foreground the Molendinar Burn ripples past the gardens of the prebendal manses that sloped down from the Drygate. The houses of High Street are seen and of the five spires in the background the centre one is that of the Old College.*

Armour's Wynd, New Wynd and Old Wynd.

The town also accommodated its rising population by filling in the gaps in the original streets.

HIGH STREET TO GLASGOW CROSS

In the sixteenth century the lower part of High Street began to be filled with a mixture of buildings, such as the house erected in 1560 at the corner of Bun's Wynd, now Nicholas Street. David Small's sketch of 1885 shows the house with its crow-stepped gable and two bow-shaped shop windows added at the beginning of the nineteenth century. The building was demolished in the 1870s as it came under the City of Glasgow Improvement Act of 1866, which made a clean sweep of most of the ancient buildings that formed the nucleus of the city.

David Small's sketch of 1885 showing house at corner of Bun's Wynd.

This sketch of the Dove House shows what was left of the house after the 1863 alter-ation. The moulded chimney-heads and crow steps had vanished. Unlike the pre-Reformation rubble-stone manses, the facade of Dove House was of close-jointed hewn stones. No structural alterations appeared to have been made at any time. The walls were 2½ feet thick. The large regularly placed windows admitted good light to every room, and the modern-looking fireplaces and other interior arrangements show the advanced state of domestic architecture in Glasgow at the close of the sixteenth century. During demolition, the crooked, stunted oak trees, which had been used for joists, were evidence of the scarcity of building timber in the district around Glasgow in 1596.

DOVE HOUSE
*

A late sixteenth-century house in High Street was the Dove House, situated on the west side of the street a few yards up from what is now George Street. It was said to be a hostelry in by-gone days and the principal inn at the time of the Royal Stuarts. The back wall fronting the inner court had a heraldic representation of a dove and the date '1596' was cut into the top of the inner court gable. Queen Victoria admired the old house when she drove up the High Street on her way to the Cathedral in 1849. Around 1863 the top storey was removed as the building was thought to be dangerous. The date stone was preserved and placed under a shop counter in the building where it remained until the house was demolished in 1900. The stone is now in the People's Palace, Glasgow Green.

Hopkirk's Land, High Street (land was a synonym for tenement). David Dale, 'the father of the cotton trade in Scotland' and a great philanthropist, started business in 1763 in the middle tenement of the sketch (John Smith & Co.). The building was early seventeenth century and stood on the east side of the High Street, just five doors from Glasgow Cross, the heart of commercial Glasgow. Dale's shop had one room, and it was there in 1783 that the Royal Bank opened its first Glasgow branch. Hopkirk's Land was demolished in 1914.

THE OLD COLLEGE

✱

Below what is now the junction of Duke Street and George Street, most of the east side of High Street was taken up by the University, which vacated its home in Rottenrow in 1459 when James, the first Lord Hamilton, gifted it a tenement in High Street and four acres of land stretching eastwards to the Molendinar Burn. Lord Hamilton made the gift on the condition that, before meals, the regents and students should pray for his soul and for those of his

This engraving by Joseph Swan shows the Old College in the High Street, c.1828

relatives. In 1467 Thomas Arthurlie added an adjacent tenement and 'croft'. A century later Queen Mary gave money, property and an additional thirteen acres on the Dow Hill to the east.

Although the University suffered during the Reformation because of its papal origins, by the early seventeenth century it had recovered until 'there was no place in Europe comparable to Glasgow . . . for a plentiful and good cheap market of all kinds of languages, arts, and sciences'. The University had by then outgrown its buildings, consisting of Auld Pedagogy, Arthurlie House and Principal's House, and after they were demolished, work on a new university began in 1632. Building, however, was interrupted by the Civil War, and it was not until 1661 that the complex making up the University, or College as it was known, was completed. Set in a heavily ornamented archway, the College gate had massive oak nail-studded doors, which were closed at night. Over the gateway were the College arms with the date 1658. After the Restoration, these were removed and the royal arms, the lion and unicorn with the initials 'C.R.2', substituted.

The Scottish Jacobean facade of the College to High Street was almost symmetrical, two storeys with an attic in the centre, three with attics at the

Old College Clock Tower

ends. The line of the eaves was continuous. Three tall chimneys topped the centrepiece gable. On the High Street frontage to the south was the Principal's House; to the north were those of the two Professors of Divinity. John Boyd and John Clerk were the Glasgow masons responsible for the building.

Behind the rusticated frontage were two quadrangles, the inner having a tower and a Dutch-style steeple 140 feet high with a gilded cock on the spear. There was no clock until 1686. The steeple was a prominent feature of old Glasgow. In the Outer Quadrangle was the Lion and Unicorn Staircase erected in 1690. Both quadrangles were paved with red sandstone.

To the south of the College buildings was the College Church, erected in 1699. To the north was a garden where later the Professors' Court was built. To the east, the grounds were open, sloping gently down to the Molendinar Burn. In the eighteenth century, a terrace walk 122 feet long and 64 feet broad was created, beyond which was a garden of seven acres. The garden was called 'the great yard'. In 1704 a physic, or botanic, garden was laid out. Not all students had access to the gardens, the privilege being confined to the sons of noblemen who were scholars. To each of this favoured class the faculty allowed 'a key to the great garden and Physic garden, providing the said privileged persons promised to allow no other the use of the said key'. Over the years an Observatory, an Examination Hall, and a Library designed by William Adam were added to the College buildings. William Stark's Hunterian Museum replaced the terrace walk.

By Victorian times the College was surrounded by some of the worst slums in Glasgow. Two streets in particular, the Havannah and the New Vennel, were the filthiest in the city. When Lord Kelvin's brother, who was on the staff of the University, contracted typhus and died, Lord Kelvin maintained the infection had come 'over the wall from the New Vennel'. He was therefore one of many who agreed that the University should move from High Street. James Smart, Superintendent of Police, condemned the site in High Street as follows: 'The College of Glasgow is situated in an old and decayed part of the city where the very poorest of the population reside and where, as is usual in such localities, there is a large number of whisky shops, little pawns and houses in which disreputable persons of both sexes are harboured. The district is one of the worst of the city, as to the character of the inhabitants. Crimes and disorders are of daily occurrence, rendering it one of the most troublesome parts of the city to the police. From the character of the district altogether, it appears to me an unfit place for a great educational institution such as the University.'

This Annan photograph shows the old house of Gilmorehill with construction
work on the University proceeding in the background. The house was built in
1802 and demolished about 1867

There had been a proposal in 1846 that a railway company would erect a
new college at Woodlands and take over the High Street buildings. Nothing
came of it, but the University did move, in the 1870s, to Gilmorehill, after
accepting an offer of £10,000 from the City of Glasgow Union Railway
Company for the Old College site.

What happened to the Old College is on a par with knocking down the
two medieval Cathedral Towers. The whole thing was cleared away around
1885. It was a crime. The slums should have been demolished and the College
kept. Even at the time of their destruction, the buildings were recognised by
distinguished architectural opinion as the finest group of seventeenth-
century buildings in Scotland. Of all the buildings demolished during the
city's 'improvement', the greatest loss of all was that of the Old College. Some
common sense did prevail – the Lion and Unicorn staircase was transferred
to Gilmorehill along with part of the old facade, which became the Pearce
Lodge.

GRAMMAR SCHOOL

*

On the opposite side of High Street from the University was the Grammar School, which was much older than the University. Although documentary evidence shows its existence only in the early fourteenth century, it is believed to have started two centuries before. With the institution of the Roman Catholic clergy in the city during the twelfth century there existed an educational establishment called the Seminary of the Canons Regular, which is regarded as the precursor of the 'Old Grammar Schule'.

An entry in the burgh minutes of 1578 is the earliest preserved record of the connection of the Town Council with the Grammar School. The entry was in the Treasurer's accounts for the cost of straw 'to theik the grammar scole'. This shows that the building had a thatched roof. When it was built is not known, but it was taken down in 1600, a new building being erected on the site in 1601.

The Grammar School was renewed in 1656 and remained in use until 1788 when the new school on the north side of George Street was occupied. Although the old school was taken down in 1874 through the operations of the City Improvement Trust, a relic is preserved that established the date of the building. It is a stone taken from the lintel of the doorway at the back, which, along with two other stones removed from the Grammar School in John Street, is built into a gable wall of the building in Elmbank Street that once housed the High School, originally the Grammar School. The lettering is in Latin but in English reads: 'The Grammar School erected by its Patrons, the Municipal Authorities and Citizens of Glasgow, for the Promotion of Literature.' In the middle is a medallion in which the city arms appear, topped by the date 1601.

WOODEN HOUSES

*

Glasgow's so-called wooden houses were stone houses with their timber balconies boarded up to increase living and shop accommodation. The wooden projections resulted in narrow streets and were frequently the cause of fires, like that of 1652 which wiped out a third of the city. The fire started in a narrow alley on the east side of the High Street and raged into Gallowgate and Trongate and down the Saltmarket as far as Bridgegate. Driven by the wind, the flames swept along the wooden fronts like a forest fire, leaving nearly a thousand families homeless.

Back and front views of the Grammar School. Originally, the building had a steeple, but when the Grammar School moved into new premises in George Street in 1788, the old schoolhouse was altered to adapt it for dwelling houses, which is when the steeple was taken down. The site of the old Grammar School was occupied partly by Ingram Street and partly by a fire station that still stands but is now used for commercial purposes.

After the fire, the Town Council forbade the erection of timber-fronted houses. Nevertheless, often the old style of building was carried on, especially in the unsanitary backlands, until there was another fire in 1677, which destroyed 136 houses and shops. This time the Council ordered that 'each persone building *de novo* on the Hie Street, or repairing, sall be obleiged to doe it by stone work from head to foot back and foir without any timber or daill except in the inset thereof which is understood to be partitions, doors, windows, presses and such lyk.'

The last surviving timber-fronted house in High Street was No. 101, built around 1652 and demolished near the end of the nineteenth century. All the other similar houses in the street were cleared in 1848.

In the middle of the eighteenth century, 75 High Street, Fiddlers' Close, was the best specimen extant of the style of building followed in the seventeenth century in the Glasgow closes. Its gable-like fronts, steep thatched roofs, crow steps, outside stairs and wooden projections that extended the living space but diminished the narrow space between the houses across the way were typical of the time. Fiddlers' Close was built around 1650 and took its name from several fiddlers who lived there. (A *close* or *closs* – an enclosed space – was originally the enclosed courtyard behind a building. Later it became a narrow lane between backlands and in the nineteenth century the common passage leading from the street to the backcourt and thus the stair.)

DUTCH-STYLE STONE-FRONTED ARCADED TENEMENTS

*

Further down High Street, near the Cross, were buildings very different from Fiddlers' Close: stone-fronted tenements, their style copied from the architecture of the Netherlands. The tall, narrow, Dutch-fronted buildings were erected in the four main streets around the Cross. A peculiarity of the buildings was the placing of the gable on the street frontage. An attractive feature was the piazzas under them, the outer line of the buildings resting upon pillars, forming a continuous arcade. The main traders in the city conducted their business under the arches, which also offered vaulted ground-floor storage cellars for merchants who came to attend the fairs to stow their goods in at night. The arches were blocked up after the 1800 Glasgow Police Act

Right.
This sketch by David Small in 1885 shows the timber-fronted 101 High Street. The building in front of it, facing High Street, is much later, possibly eighteenth century.

described them as 'Receptacles for Thieves, Pickpockets and idle and disorderly Persons'. It was recommended that the shops be advanced to fill the area of the piazzas. Two of the last arcaded tenements to survive stood on the west side of High Street, a short distance from the Tolbooth.

At the foot of High Street stood the city Cross – the one that superseded the ancient Cross at the intersection of Rottenrow and Drygate. Of what form it took there is no authentic record. At the beginning of the seventeenth century, however, the guardhouse was built against or round it, and when the guardhouse was removed farther west in 1659, the Cross was found to be so ruined that it was also removed. A council minute of 1 October 1659 confirms this.

WEST ALONG TRONGATE

Trongate expanded westwards very slowly, and by the beginning of the seventeenth century had stretched no farther than the mouth of the Old Wynd, a short distance from the Cross. Fifty years later, it had only reached

Left.
William Simpson's watercolour shows a somewhat romanticised view of Fiddlers' Close in the 1840s by which time it had come down in the world. Until the close of the seventeenth century it was the 'Buchanan Street of Georgian Glasgow', as a Victorian reporter put it. It was the home of some of Glasgow's most fashionable shops and highly respectable middle-class people tenanted the houses. By the early nineteenth century, however, impoverished Irish occupied the dwellings, and as they paid no rent and therefore could not be ejected, Fiddlers' Close became a dirty, verminous, grossly overcrowded slum, and in 1848 the Dean of Guild Court ordered it to be demolished. Another reason for the houses being removed was that the area of the city from the Cross northwards was notorious for overcrowding and had been earmarked as being the principal rendezvous of the scum and villains of the city. Only part of Fiddlers' Close was demolished, most of it surviving until 1878 when the Gas Showroom replaced it.

Apparently when the first Irishman found his way into the locality, the Scottish inhabitants tolerated him only because he had agreed to keep the close clean, for which he was paid a pittance. He and his family, however, were treated like pariahs and there was no interaction between them and their neighbours.

A detail worth pointing out in the illustration is that under the stair on the right is a well by which the Old Glasgow Water Company supplied water to the building.

*High Street c. 1868. The last of the arcaded tenements photographed before
their demolition in the mid-1870s. The gabled building shows the famous piazzas
that once continued right along the buildings on the main streets. These piazzas were
much admired by Daniel Defoe and other eighteenth-century visitors to Glasgow.
Glasgow, wrote Defoe, 'is a large, stately, and well-built city, standing on a plain in the
manner four-square; and the four principal streets are the fairest for breadth and the
finest built that I have ever seen in one city altogether. The houses are all of stone, and
generally uniform in height as well as in front. The lower storeys, for the most part,
stand on vast square Doric columns, with arches, which open into the shops adding to
the strength as well as beauty of the building. In a word, 'tis one of the cleanliest, most
beautiful, and best built cities in Great Britain.' Defoe must have been describing the
buildings when he spoke of cleanliness, as in Glasgow, at the beginning of the
eighteenth century, it was extremely rudimentary, the night watchmen
devoting two hours twice a week to the job.*

Opposite.
Thatched malt barn and kiln at the foot of Mitchell Street.

Stockwell Street, the city's western extremity. The West Port, which marked the boundary, had been moved from the Old Wynd to Stockwell Street in 1588. Outside the gate was a cattle market held on the open road.

Although the city boundary to the west was at the head of Stockwell Street, there were houses, barns and kilns scattered along the roadside beyond the West Port. There was also a thatched hostelry for drovers and a farmhouse flanked by byres and outhouses. Cows were milked in front of the farmhouse. The last of these old buildings to disappear was a thatched malt barn and kiln that stood back from the roadway at the foot of Mitchell Street. Built in the sixteenth century, it was taken down about 1830.

TOLBOOTH
*

In the Trongate, just round the corner from the High Street's arcaded buildings, was another of Glasgow's ancient buildings that should never have been

demolished, the municipal building and jail erected in 1626. Although not on a par with knocking down the Cathedral's medieval Towers or the Old College, the building should have been preserved, as it was a significant part of Glasgow's past.

In Glasgow, a tolbooth at the Cross is mentioned as early as 1454. Little is known about this structure other than documents calling it 'Pretorium' and that booths, or shops, occupied its street-level accommodation, the rents going towards maintaining the property and nothing else.

What appears to be the first municipal building became unsuitable and was taken down. The 'grund stane' of a new building was laid on 15 March 1626, and eight months later the five-storey building, complete with 126-feet-high steeple, became Glasgow's civic centre and prison. A visitor described the building as 'a very sumptuous, regulated, uniform fabric, large and lofty, most industriously and artificially carved from the very foundation to the superstructure, to the great admiration of strangers and is without exception, the paragon of beauty in the west.'

A paragon of beauty the building may have been, but it had a defect. The entrance to the council chamber, on the floor above the street, was too small, which meant that a large outside stair had to be added.

Despite the addition of a town hall in 1740 and an extension to it in 1758, the Tolbooth was inadequate as a civic centre, so in 1814 the jail, court, council chambers, etc, moved to new quarters at the foot of the Saltmarket designed by William Stark.

In 1814 architect David Hamilton rebuilt the Tolbooth in a Gothic style meant to resemble the original. Why it was necessary to knock an ancient building down and build another to resemble it defies logic. Logic, however, was rarely in evidence through the centuries when Glasgow's leaders so cavalierly forfeited its ancient buildings. Luckily, the steeple narrowly escaped demolition.

When David Hamilton's Tolbooth was demolished in the mid-1920s, the steeple was again under threat of demolition, this time to ease the flow of traffic into High Street. Fortunately, it got another stay of execution, the road being widened, leaving the steeple marooned on its island.

Left.
The oldest house in Trongate, sketched by David Small in 1885, nine years before it was demolished. For generations the house was known as the oldest house in the street. Built in 1591, it was a landmark for 306 years. Being a detached house it escaped the two great fires. Architecturally it was similar to the Dove House in High Street, erected in 1595. Both houses had a date stone.

*The old Tolbooth and steeple. Although this illustration shows the Tolbooth to
have a double outside staircase, the one added when it was discovered that the entrance
to the council chamber on the floor above the street was too small was only a
single staircase. The double one was introduced in 1792.*

Opposite.
David Hamilton's Tolbooth of 1814, built to resemble the building it replaced.

HUTCHESONS' HOSPITAL
✳

In 1641, Thomas Hutcheson laid the foundation stone of another of Glasgow's
landmark buildings, Hutchesons' Hospital in the Trongate. Brothers George
and Thomas Hutcheson founded the hall, or hospital as it was called, in 1639
to provide shelter for 'poore, aigit and decreppit men' and a school for 'twelve

Tolbooth Steeple,
Glasgow Cross

mail children, indigent orphanes or utheres of like condition'. Those named Hutcheson or Herbertson had preference. The boys' furnishings were austerely simple: ten hair blankets, seven pairs of sheets and five chaff bolsters. Their schoolmaster was provided with a 'great keeking glass', something the boys had to do without when dressing themselves in the purple uniform that made them so conspicuous as they marched to the Tron Church twice each Sunday. Boys and pensioners lived on a diet of porridge and herrings daily, with kail being served every second day. Beef appeared only once a month, but every day each inmate, young or old, received four pints of ale. So that they might get the full benefit of their education, the boys had no house duties imposed on them.

Pensioners and scholars, however, occupied the Hospital only at intervals. Because of the desirability of its location, it was more expedient to convert it into shops and warehouses that were let at high rents to raise a much larger income for charitable purposes. Consequently, by the end of the eighteenth century the function of the Hospital was largely to pay pensions to the needy. As the city expanded westwards, the Hospital sold its property and feued a street, using the proceeds to build a new hall as the old one was crumbling. The buildings were demolished in May 1795 and Hutcheson Street was formed.

EAST ALONG GALLOWGATE

Just as Trongate had expanded very little westwards by the middle of the seventeenth century, Gallowgate had expanded very little eastwards. It had reached only as far as the East Port at Dovehill, not far from the Cross. On the north beyond the East Port was only a narrow hedge-lined country road

Front and back views of Hutchesons' Hospital in Trongate, published in Views & Notices of Glasgow in Former Times. *By the time Hutchesons' Hospital was built, the style of Glasgow's architecture was changing, with long, low facades replacing the vertical emphasis. The Hospital, a two-storey block, had a tall steeple behind a nine-bay facade. To the rear, the building was L-shaped, stretching out behind with circular stair towers. Glasgow's first historian, M'Ure, described it as 'a very handsome building of ashler work, 'tis not high but beautiful . . . . North of the hospital there are very pleasant and delectable gardens that are well kept and much resorted to for the recreation of walking in them.' The buildings contained six dormitories for the pensioners, another for the boys, two apartments for the schoolmaster, a schoolroom, a joint sitting room, a kitchen and a hall.*

leading to the old village of Camlachie. Between the port and the Cross, the Molendinar Burn crossed the street.

Gallowgate had suffered in the two disastrous fires, but some of the old crow-stepped buildings and wooden houses survived until the nineteenth century. Of these one was a fine stone building with three crow-stepped gables. This was described in 1736 as being 'the great and stately lodging belonging to Thomas Orr with a fine garden at the head thereof and a well in the close, very useful to the tenants and the neighbourhood.' The tenement was removed in 1854 during alterations to the north side of Gallowgate. Entered through the three-gabled building was a close, the houses of which were largely built of wood.

Along with soap-making, an industry that began Glasgow's manufacturing and commercial prosperity was sugar refining. Before 1651, there had been attempts at it, but it was not until 1667 that the first successful refinery, the Wester Sugar House, was set up in Candleriggs and Bell's Wynd. Two years later, the Easter Sugar House was established on the south side of Gallowgate. Eventually there were at least five sugar houses in the city, all of which diversified into the distillation of rum.

THE OLD BURNT BARNS INN
*

Slightly to the south of the Gallowgate stood the Old Burnt Barns Inn, established in 1679. It was built at the corner of one of the main avenues leading from the south to the city. The line of what is now London Road was then known as Craignestock Lone and was a mere country road leading to Dalmarnock. The narrow alley by which it was joined to the Gallowgate was called St Mungo's Lane (it was opposite the site of the Chapel of Little Saint Mungo). The only access to the city from the east in this district was by the Gallowgate and Craignestock Lone, and the Burnt Barns Inn was placed at a spot where it was sure to intercept wayfarers on their road to or from Rutherglen and the south.

William Simpson's watercolour of the Orr family's three-gabled tenement on the north side of Gallowgate. The gables indicate that the building is much older than those beside it.

Overleaf.
William Simpson's watercolour of the old close, through from the gabled tenement belonging to the Orr family, shows just how narrow the alleys were and how far the wooden top storeys of the houses projected.

Previous page.
The Sugar House Close, No. 138 Gallowgate. William Simpson's watercolour gives a
view looking north through the passage to the Gallowgate. Although when Simpson
painted his picture in the early 1840s the Easter Sugar House was in a sorry state, it
showed it had been a substantial, gabled stone building. The building was condemned
in 1848 and removed a few years later.

Above.
David Small's drawing of the Old Burnt Barns Inn in Craignestock Lone,
which became Great Hamilton Street and is now London Road.

Right.
Gallowgate, photographed by Thomas Annan just before the old houses were
demolished in the second half of the nineteenth century. The photograph shows a mix
of buildings. On the right, a new tenement adjoins a two-storey building that joins a
narrow three-storey crow-stepped building, which looks as if it might have had a
thatched roof at one time. Note the flat window in the roof, an early version of a
velux window. Compared to its neighbours, its roof looks new. Beside the narrow
building is one of three storeys and an attic.

58

A row of thatched houses standing on the west side of St Mungo's Lane was called the Burnt Barns, apparently because there were grain barns on the site which were burnt in 1668. It is supposed that that is how the inn got its name. While the Old Burnt Barns Inn is no more, the name lives on in the pub built on the same spot.

SOUTH TO THE RIVER

SALTMARKET
*

The continuation of High Street, Saltmarket, linked Glasgow Cross to the head of Bridgegate, which led to the Glasgow Bridge. Known originally as Walcargate, the street had been one of the chief thoroughfares in Glasgow since 1100. While the burgh in ancient times was clustered around the Cathedral on the summit of the hill, it was necessary that the inhabitants should have a direct line of communication with the River Clyde from which they drew their principal food supply – fish. The southern boundary of the city was at the foot of Walcargate. About 1650 the name of the street was changed to Saltmarket. In 1668, the title deeds of property on the east side of the Saltmarket declared that 'the owners shall have the privilege of fishing in the Molendinar Burn'.

After the disastrous fire of 1652, which destroyed most of Saltmarket, the street was largely rebuilt with stone-fronted arcaded buildings in the same Dutch style as those in High Street. In these buildings, the merchants, often very wealthy, lived in very homely fashion. The shops, or business premises, were one or two small, low-roofed and dimly lit rooms on the street level, the merchants living on the floors above.

The great and wealthy once lived in Saltmarket. Provost Gibson's house, Gibson's Land, with its eighteen stately pillars, was the grandest of all the dwellings. After the 1677 fire, Walter Gibson had rebuilt on his plot at the northeast corner of Gibson's Wynd, Sir William Bruce, the architect of Holyrood, designing his magnificent new home. Two disasters befell it. Over the centuries it was sublet and subdivided until it belonged to various owners who made so many alterations that the building collapsed in 1814. Although nine families were living there, only one person died. In 1823 the tenement again collapsed and although the inhabitants had been warned two days before, again a life was lost. Gibson's Wynd became Princes Street, which became Parnie Street.

WOODEN HOUSES
*

A few post-Reformation timber-fronted houses that survived the 1625 fire, the 1677 fire and the ravages of time and weather existed in the Saltmarket until the 1870s when they were swept away in the city improvements. One was 28 Saltmarket, built around 1570. The building was constructed in a similar fashion to 101 High Street, but the staircase was curious. Starting from the bottom of the southeast gable, it ran diagonally across the whole of the front elevation until it reached the top flat landing of the southwest gable, being screened throughout its whole length by the projecting timber front. The first flight of steps was entirely of stone, as were the walls of the street flat, but all the staircase above the first landing was of wood.

Another of the old timber-fronted lands to survive was 77 Saltmarket. Houses of this kind were erected because of the cheapness of the materials and to economise on ground space. To achieve this, beams were projected from the first storey and an outshot and additional structure raised upon them, which obstructed ventilation, giving an inconvenient, cold and comfortless dwelling. When in a close, houses of this kind were generally occupied by working people or by those who rented a small shop in the front street and lodged themselves in one of the fragile-looking tenements behind.

DOWHILL'S LAND
*

Dowhill's Land in Saltmarket, once the town residence of the Andersons of Dowhill, was possibly the best of the Dutch-fronted buildings in the city. The fine old crow-stepped tenement was described in the title deeds as 'that great fore high tenement in Saltmarket Street of Glasgow commonly called Dowhill's Land'. John Anderson was Provost of Glasgow from 1655 to 1658. The last of Glasgow's old timber-fronted lands, Robb's Close, 122 Saltmarket, was entered through a 'yett' (a narrow opening) in Dowhill's Land. Both Dowhill's Land and Robb's Close were demolished in the 1870s.

SILVERCRAIG'S LAND
*

An example of the horizontal style of building adopted in Glasgow in the seventeenth century was Silvercraig's Land at the foot of Saltmarket on the east side. Silvercraig's Land, built by Robert Campbell of Silvercraigs, was

Above.
Painting by Thomas Fairbairn, c. 1849, of 77 Saltmarket, showing houses 'reared
up of timber and deall boards'. That buildings of this type survived for over 300 years
is extraordinary. While the buildings in the illustration have glazed windows,
originally the window openings had sliding shutters, one of which remains
in the gable of the middle house.

Left.
The close at 28 Saltmarket, drawn by David Small. For a tenement constructed
of such perishable materials to survive in a place that had been devastated by fires was
incredible, as was the fact that it went on to endure the ravages of time and weather
and development, the fate of nearly all the contemporary buildings of a similar
style that escaped the fires.

Overleaf Left.
Dowhill's Land, Saltmarket, the fine old tenement built for the Andersons of Dowhill.

Overleaf right.
Looking down Robb's Close, drawn by David Small. The timber overhang
of the top storeys of the buildings looks picturesque.

Silvercraig's Land was two storeys high with attics. On its front was a large stone with the national arms of Scotland below which were two shields representing the Argyll family and the houses of Campbell and Stewart.

famous for being the house where Oliver Cromwell lodged when he was in Glasgow in 1650. It was there he met Zachary Boyd, minister of the Barony, and other local dignitaries. When the City Improvement Trust tore down the building, the large room where Cromwell had held his meetings was being used as an auction hall and the building had become a breeding ground of vice and disease because of overcrowding. The model tenements of workmen's dwelling houses erected by the City Improvement Trust in 1887 replaced Silvercraig's Land.

BRIDGEGATE

Bridgegate forked from the west side of Saltmarket to connect with Glasgow Bridge. Until the early 1700s, the street was the most fashionable in the city and contained the residences of the city's leading citizens.

*Drawing by David Small of the famous Ship Bank at the corner
of Bridgegate and Saltmarket.*

THE SHIP BANK

✳

Provost Bell had a house built at the corner of Bridgegate and Saltmarket around 1640, and King James VII, when Duke of York, lived in it when he visited Glasgow. An item of expenditure connected with the visit consisted of £860 'for provisions in the proveistis hous the tyme the Duke was there and theis that were with him'.

A century later, Provost Bell's house became the original office of Glasgow's first bank. The Glasgow and Ship Bank opened in 1750 and became popularly known as the Ship Bank as its bank notes bore a picture of a ship. West Highlanders held the notes in great esteem, preferring them to any others. The Ship Bank remained in the Saltmarket/Bridgegate building for twenty-six years and then moved to the Trongate. Later the Ship Bank and the Thistle Bank amalgamated to become the Union Bank. When the Ship

Bank moved from its first home, the building was divided among various tenants. The area was already falling from its former fashionable position.

The quaint old building survived until 1904 when the Ship Bank Building replaced it. There is a reminder, however, of the old Ship Bank in the present Ship Bank Building. The Ship Bank Tavern on the ground floor has etched glass windows depicting how the seventeenth-century building looked.

THE MERCHANTS HOUSE

*

The most important building in Bridgegate, and the one giving the street its fashionable address, was the Merchants House, built in 1659 on the north side.

If more of Glasgow's records had survived, we might have a clearer idea of how and when the merchants' guild began. It is known, however, that the merchants were an established, though unofficial, institution long before the trades people began to organise themselves into separate guilds to try to get fair play in the burgh's administration, which was dominated by the merchants who excluded craftsmen from their guild.

The dominance of the merchants came to an end in 1605 when the Merchants House and Trades House were formed simultaneously by the famous Letter of Guildry, the result of arbitration to settle the constant disputes between craftsmen and merchants over rank, precedence and trading privileges. The Letter defined the position of each party with the election of a Dean of Guild (merchants) and a Deacon Convener (craftsmen), each with a seat on the town council. A Dean of Guild's Court was created, which originally dealt with all matters concering the Merchants House but latterly was associated with the city's planning and building matters.

A Merchants' Hospital had been set up in Bridgegate in 1601. (Then a hospital was not primarily a place for the sick, it was an almshouse for pensioners who had no other home.) Although at first the Hospital provided shelter, most assistance was given by way of pensions or grants paid to 'decayed' merchants or widows and daughters in distress who were living elsewhere in the town.

In 1659 the merchants rebuilt the decaying hospital in the Bridgegate, reputedly to a design by Sir William Bruce. Fronting the street, the new Merchants House was almost identical to Hutchesons' Hospital – two storeys with a steeple behind a long, low, nine-bay symmetrical facade. Columns and strapwork ornamented the central doorway, and pediments topped the upper

The Merchant's House, Bridgegate, c. 1659.

floor windows. The 164-foot-high steeple was described as 'being of curious architecture with three battlements above one another and a curious clock of molten brass, the spire of which has a ship of copper in place of a weather-cock'.

The guildhall, lit by fourteen windows, occupied the whole of the building's upper floor. There was also accommodation for poor old men. Behind was a large flower garden surrounded by a nine-foot wall. All the great assemblies and balls were held in the Merchants House.

The merchants stayed in their Bridgegate home until they sold it in 1817 with the stipulation that the steeple must be preserved as it was 'an ornament to the city', which it is to this day.

BLYTHSWOOD TOWN HOUSE

*

Colin Campbell of Blythswood's town residence on the south side of Bridgegate, built in 1660, was similar in style to the nearby Merchants House, except that the facade had eleven bays and was asymmetrical. Blythswoods

The Blythswood town house of Colin Campbell.

occupied the building, which had a large garden behind, until the end of the eighteenth century. It was sold in 1802, and eventually some of the railway lines converging on St Enoch Station covered its site.

STOCKWELL STREET
*

Stockwell Street, which started life as Fishergate, was a rural locality for a long time. Trees shaded the houses, many of them quaint buildings with thatched roofs, those on the west side having gardens and open country behind them.

At the corner of Stockwell and Great Clyde Street (Clyde Street now) was a gabled tenement, built in 1668, which replaced three small houses with 'yeards' that had existed since 1599. From 1757 to 1780, when Glasgow became an independent port, the tenement served as the Custom House of Glasgow. After 1780 the Custom House moved to Smithfield, opposite the present Oswald Street, then to the west side of St Enoch Square where it remained until 1840 when a new Custom House was erected in Clyde Street near the Jamaica Bridge. The Stockwell house was removed to make way for a tenement called Victoria Buildings, also gone.

Idealised watercolour by Andrew Donaldson of dwellings in Stockwell Street, c. 1817.

Corner of Stockwell and Great Clyde Street from a watercolour by William Simpson. The gabled end of the building faced the river.

The last seventeenth-century tenement in Glasgow, 24 Stockwell Street.

LAST SEVENTEENTH-CENTURY
TENEMENT IN THE CITY
*

The last surviving seventeenth-century tenement in the city was 24 Stockwell Street. Dating from 1678, the building went through various uses in its long life. Many famous persons lodged beneath its roof. One was 'The Gentle Lochiel', who prevented Glasgow from being sacked by Prince Charlie Edward Stuart and his Jacobites when they occupied the town in December 1745. After HM Customs vacated the building, Garrick's Temperance Coffee House and Commercial Lodgings, later shortened to the Garrick Temperance Hotel, took it over. Jenny Lind, the famous Swedish singer, stayed there in 1847 when she gave concerts in the city.

Although at some time in the nineteenth century the street elevation had been spoiled by the removal of two of the dormer windows, the building retained its seventeenth-century appearance. The dormers were similar to those on the Merchants House and the first Hutchesons' Hospital. Despite alterations internally over the centuries, much of the panelling and many of the original fittings remained until the building was demolished in 1975. This followed the clearance of the area with the demolition of St Enoch Station. A car park had been created, and the seventeenth-century building was sacrificed to make an entrance to it. Strangely, the building had been removed from the listed register before demolition. That the building should have been demolished in the 1970s, when the council was meant to be more enlightened in its attitude towards ancient buildings, was ironic, as it had survived the clearance of the area in the 1860s to allow for the introduction of a new railway line across the Clyde to St Enoch Square.

GLASGOW BEFORE THE UNION

While by 1672 Glasgow was the second city in Scotland, the seventeenth century closed amid gloom and ruin. In 1695 the Scottish parliament decided to establish a colony in Central America that would obtain a share in the Pacific trade. In 1698 five ships sailed from Leith to establish the colony on the Isthmus of Darien. The first expedition ended in disaster, as did the second, which sailed from the Clyde in 1699. Half of all Scotland's capital was lost, and two thousand colonists died. Glasgow lost a fortune in money and in human lives.

The Scots blamed the Darian fiasco on the English parliament, which, afraid that the venture would hurt the supremacy of the powerful East India Company, gave orders that the colony should not be allowed to trade with English colonies or English ships. In addition, the Spaniards, who looked on the region as belonging to them, realised that England would not defend the Scottish colony and attacked it. No aid was given from the English governors in the Bahamas. The treatment of the Darien expedition and other matters, like the Act of Succession, brought Scotland and England to the verge of civil war, forcing a parliamentary union between the two countries in 1707. After the Union, Scotland received compensation for the Darien scheme.

CHAPTER 3
FROM MERCHANT CITY
TO VICTORIAN CITY
1707–1837

*

BENEFITS OF THE UNION

Despite the Union guaranteeing Scotland equal trading rights with England, strangely, Glasgow, the city that profited more than any other from the Union, violently opposed it, with the Articles of Union being burned at the Cross. There was a general call to arms, there were riots and the provost had to flee for his life. It was feared that much of the city's trade with the Continent would be lost and that much of Scotland's wealth would end up in London when the parliament was based there.

After the initial disturbances, almost from the day the Act of Union was signed, Glasgow merchants seized the opportunities thrown open to them and began the trade in sugar and tobacco on which the fortunes of the city were to be founded.

At the time of the Union in 1707, Scotland owned only 215 ships. Leith had 35, Glasgow 13 and the Clyde ports 8. By 1712, the number of Scottish ships was 1,123. Leith had 45, Glasgow 46 and the Clyde ports 149.

While Scotland's merchants rejoiced in being able to trade in areas previously prohibited, the English ports of Bristol, London, Liverpool and Whitehaven resented the Scottish incursion into their territory, especially as the Clyde estuary was the most convenient outlet in Britain for trading with America. Glasgow's ships had a start on their English rivals of a month or six weeks as they did not have to fight their way through the English Channel, frequently blocked with privateers and French and Spanish warships, Britain often being at war in the eighteenth century. By the time the English ships had cleared the channel, Glasgow's ships were often at Virginia. The quicker voyage also saved on food and wages to the crew and wear and tear on the ship. (The Virginia colony should not be identified with today's state of

Virginia. It ran in a great semicircle round the New England colonies from the Virginia Atlantic Coast to Lake Erie and was governed from Williamsburg.)

The English ports protested to the government that they were almost stripped of their tobacco trade and accused Glasgow of carrying off their traffic by unfair means. They accused Glasgow of evading the payment of duty on the tobacco it imported. When Treasury officials were sent to Glasgow to investigate, however, they found nothing wrong and declared that the complaints by the English ports had been made out of envy. Nevertheless, the complaints continued and various prohibitive measures were imposed involving Glasgow's merchants in vexatious lawsuits, so for a time the tobacco trade declined.

After 1735, however, when the English obstructions had failed, Glasgow's tobacco trade soared, and by 1755 it was the biggest tobacco-importing city in Britain. Only a small amount of the tobacco imported was consumed or processed locally, the bulk being exported to Europe. In return for the merchandise from abroad, Glasgow exported leather, soap, glass and linen, providing new home industries.

Glasgow's merchants involved in the tobacco trade were nicknamed 'the tobacco lords'. They became immensely rich and strutted about the 'plain-stanes' (pavement) in front of the Exchange in the Trongate dressed in scarlet cloaks, powdered wigs and cocked hats. They claimed the exclusive right to walk on the pavement and were so full of their own importance that none outside their circle was allowed to approach them without invitation. William Cunningham, Alexander Speirs, John Glassford and James Ritchie were the greatest of the tobacco lords.

THE END OF THE TOBACCO TRADE

In 1775 the American War of Independence ended the direct tobacco trade between Glasgow and the American colonies, ruining some tobacco firms as the colonies repudiated their debt. Others suffered embarrassments but, having diversified their interests, their investments were spread widely. There was not a total collapse of the trade because many of the tobacco shipments did not come directly from the American colonies but, along with sugar and other commodities, via the Caribbean.

Arrogant they may have been, but the tobacco lords, or Virginia dons as they liked to call themselves, did much for the city by giving it ships, port facilities and financial, commercial and social advancement. They also created the first major expansion of the medieval city. There was, however, a dark side to some of them. They transported African slaves to the Caribbean plantations.

With the decline in the tobacco trade, many of Glasgow's merchants concentrated on the West Indian trade and the textile industry, the city having long been manufacturing plaids, muslins, linen and woollen goods. While for some years the West Indian trade prospered, the outbreak of the Napoleonic Wars brought it to a standstill, making 1793 one of the blackest years in Glasgow's commercial history, with bank failures and bankruptcies. Those who had focused on the textile industry, however, were more fortunate. In 1780 James Monteith of Anderston hit on an inexpensive way of weaving imitation Indian muslin wholly of cotton. Others rushed to follow his lead, and as early as 1787 there were at least nineteen mills operating alongside fast-running streams in the West of Scotland. The tobacco business, the failure of the banks, and even the wars, were set aside. Cotton was king, creating another wave of fortune making, only this time manufacturers, rather than traders, acquired the wealth.

While fortunes were made from the textile industry, it was not without problems. Wage cuts resulted in a mass withdrawal of labour, ending in bloodshed in 1787 when the Calton weavers rioted, wrecking the looms of working weavers and stoning the magistrates and town officers when they intervened. The military was called in and after the Riot Act was read, soldiers fired their muskets, killing three weavers and wounding others. The episode happened near the Drygate Bridge.

TOWNSCAPE

Street development was slow in Glasgow at the beginning of the eighteenth century, activity being confined to the built-up area, like the extension of Saltmarket in 1711. Although Bell Street, the western end of Bell's Wynd, had been created in 1710, it was ten years before another new street appeared – King Street, aligning with Candleriggs. Two years later, Princes Street (now Parnie Street) was opened, running at right angles from King Street to Saltmarket.

By 1727, conical street lamps fuelled by rapeseed and hemp oil had been put up in the High Street, Saltmarket and Bridgegate, but the dark wynds remained unlit. In 1780, as a reward for the formation of a pavement by the

*David Small's sketch of 1885 shows an early building in King Street, McNair's Land,
certainly one of the finest tenement in the city with expensive, but bizarre, decoration.
The keystones of the arches had faces similar to those of the Town Hall and each was
different from its neighbour. The sketch clearly shows two of the masks, the others
having vanished through time. Robert McNair, a grocer and general dealer, took the
unusual step of taking his wife into partnership, the firm being known as 'Robert
McNair and Jean Holmes, in Company'. McNair and his wife were eccentric and went
about their business wearing wigs and powder. She fluttered about the shop dressed in
fine silk gowns. Their grocery shop in the Trongate had two bow windows 'and a bright
green painted exterior'. McNair had an unashamed style of advertising and never
missed a trick when it came to getting one over on his competitors. Eccentric he may
have been, but he made a fortune and at the time of his death was the largest owner of
house property in Glasgow. In 1783 Frazer's Dancing Hall occupied one of the flats and
was the principal school of etiquette in the city. About the same time the first public
billiard table in the city was kept in a small, ill-lit back room in the building. McNair's
Land, sometimes known as McNair's Back Land as there was an access to it
through the close beside his shop in Trongate, was demolished in 1900.*

A railinged St Enoch Square with the handsome Adam-style Surgeons' Hall on the left, the Customs House on the right and in the centre the church designed by J. Jaffrey that opened in 1782. The Faculty of Physicians and Surgeons remained in St Enoch's Square until 1862 when it moved to its present home in St Vincent Street. Mansions further enhanced the distinguished quadrangle. The east side of St Enoch Square vanished to make way for St Enoch Station in the 1860s.

local proprietors between the Cross and Stockwell Street, the first street lights were placed on the south side of Trongate. Gas streetlights were introduced on 15 September 1818.

When the West Port was taken down in 1751, the city mushroomed westwards, and by 1775 eleven streets had been created in that direction. They were: Virginia (1753), Argyle, Jamaica and Clyde (1761), Miller (1762), Queen (1766), Howard (1768), Ingram, Maxwell and Dunlop (1772) and Buchanan (1770s). St Enoch Square, laid out in 1768, had a church in the centre and a grassy enclosure where sheep grazed and volunteers paraded.

The next batch of streets created were John (1785), Glassford (1786), Brunswick, Hutcheson and Wilson (1786), Cochrane, Frederick, Hanover, Montrose (1787), George (1792) and Garth (1793). Albion and Union came in 1802. George Square, or George's as it was called at first, was laid out in 1782. It was originally a piece of marshy land called Meadowflats. At the beginning of the nineteenth century the centre was a green where sheep grazed surrounded by a four-feet railing with a gate facing Miller Street.

George Square, as engraved by Joseph Swan in the 1820s. The houses on the north side were very grand and consisted of two rows of buildings, three storeys high, separated by North Hanover Street. On the eastern side was an uninterrupted row of good plain houses with double flights of steps in front. On the south side, the houses were handsome although not so grand as those on the north side, which had fluted Corinthian pilasters. The west side was described as having the appearance of a range of soldiers' barracks or a cotton mill. By the 1820s, the centre of the square was laid out with trees, shrubbery and flowers, intersected by numerous gravel walks. The only remnant of the original square is the Millennium Hotel, which embodies one of the two terraces of 1807–18 that occupied the north side. When the terrace was converted into the North British Hotel in 1903 an extra storey and attic were added.

The streets north of Trongate were referred to as Glasgow's 'New Town', which, with Ingram Street as its spine, was mainly classical in style, with wide streets and squares. While north of Ingram Street, the New Town was laid out to a gridiron pattern, development to the south was disjointed with streets being laid out individually along the medieval riggs (long narrow strips of ground) running north from Trongate.

Street vistas were closed by major buildings: Ingram Street by the Cunningham Mansion (later the Royal Exchange), Virginia Street by the

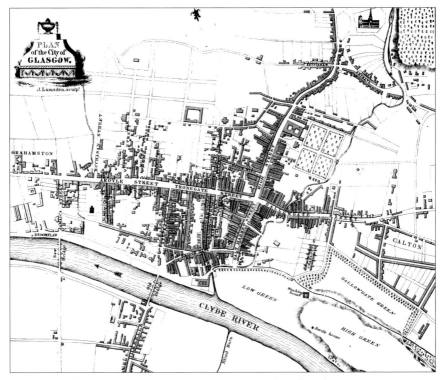

Taken from a survey by John McArthur, published in The Glasgow Magazine
and Review *in 1783, this plan of the city of Glasgow shows the extent of the town at the
close of the American War. At the western extremity is the suburb of Grahamston and
the straggling wood-yards and workshops about the Broomielaw. The upper part of
Jamaica Street appears. Newly formed Buchanan Street has only one house, in front
of which runs St Enoch's Burn. St Enoch Church has been built and the square
laid out but not built on. Queen Street is lined with villas, as is Miller Street.
Above Ingram Street, shown as straightened, but not marked, is vacant ground.
To the east, there is much vacant space around the Gallowgate. The villas
of Charlotte Street appear and to their left, standing alone,
is St Andrew's Church.*

Virginia Mansion, Ingram Street by the Star Inn and Buchanan Street by St
Enoch's Church. By the early part of the nineteenth century, Hutcheson
Street was closed by the new Hutchesons' Hospital, George Street by St
George's Tron Church and Garth Street by the Trades House at one end and
the Merchants House at the other.

Of the New Town tenements, Spreull's Land, 182 Trongate, was the most
significant to survive until comparatively recent times. Built in 1784 by an
unknown architect on the site originally occupied by a tenement standing

North side of Trongate around 1770, drawn by R. Paul. On the right is the Tolbooth steeple, the former Town House, newly opened as the Tontine Hotel. The statue of 'King Billy' was gifted to the city in 1736. To the left is the Tron Steeple. The site of Glasgow Cross, removed in 1659, is marked by inset paving in the centre of the street.

Right.
The oval spiral hanging stair of Spreull's Land, Trongate, shortly before the building was demolished.

between the famous Shawfield Mansion and Hutchesons' Hospital, it had a wide arched pend leading to the central stair and a court behind. (A pend was a wide passage through a building to allow vehicular access to the back court.) Spreull's Land was designed with shops on the ground floor and superior dwelling houses on the three upper floors. Each upper floor had two flats of five main apartments, a large lobby and various smaller rooms. The drawing rooms, situated at the back of the building, overlooked the court. No

This engraving by Joseph Swan shows the Jamaica Bridge of 1776, designed by William Mylne, architect of Edinburgh's North Bridge. This Jamaica Bridge, which had a most awkward humpback, was about 500 feet long and 32 feet wide and had seven arches. It was often called the 'Bonny Brig' and had distinctive circular holes, like portholes, through the haunches over the piers that were meant to carry off excess flood waters. The foreground of Swan's picture shows a bustling Broomielaw and crowded shipping. To the left is Clyde Street and across the river is Carlton Place and Gorbals Church.

such tenement had been built in Glasgow before, and its outstanding feature, a spiral hanging 'well' staircase, drew sightseers from far and near. (A hanging stair is one where the steps are built into the outer wall and are otherwise unsupported.) In 1840 the *Glasgow Herald* moved a printing press into a former Methodist chapel in the back part of the building. Like so many of its neighbours, Spreull's Land was a victim of supposed progress and was demolished as late as 1987.

Glasgow's growth westwards created a need for a river crossing at the west end of the city, and the foundation stone of the first Jamaica Bridge, also known as Glasgow Bridge and Broomielaw Bridge, was laid in 1776 by Provost George Murdoch. On 2 January 1772, the first vehicle, the Greenock stagecoach, passed over the bridge although the parapets were not yet built.

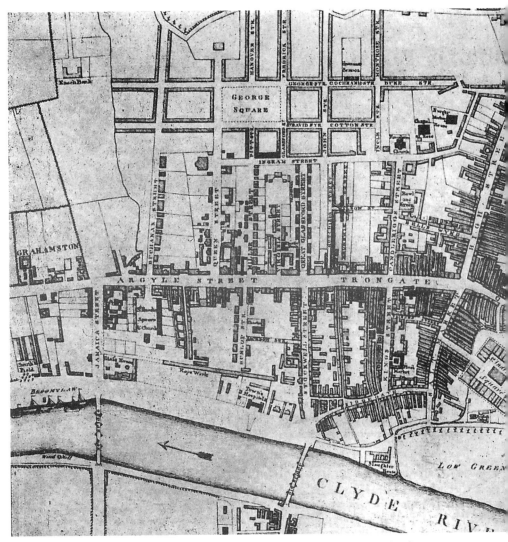

Map of Glasgow in 1796. When compared to the map of 1783, the east side of Buchanan Street has been filled with villas and the vacant ground above Ingram Street contains George Square and streets such as Duke, George, Frederick and Hanover, names inspired by the Hanoverian royal family. St Enoch Square is beginning to fill up, as is St Andrew's Square to the east.

As the bridge quickly became incapable of coping with the volume of traffic crossing it, it was decided to replace it, and the foundation stone of a new bridge designed by Thomas Telford was laid in 1833. Three years later, it was opened. Telford's Bridge was replaced in 1899 using as far as possible the materials of the old bridge, like its granite facings and balustrades.

NORTH SIDE OF ARGYLE STREET BETWEEN MILLER STREET AND HOPE STREET AT THE END OF THE EIGHTEENTH CENTURY

*

Miller Street to Queen Street

*

To the right is a kiln that formed three sides of a quadrangle. Next is the house of
Mr Miller, after whom Miller Street was named. After that is the opening to Miller
Street. The tall building to its west is newly built. Beside it is a humble little cottage set
back from the road. The handsome building near the cottage is the mansion house of
a merchant, Mr McColl, built about 1777. Queen Street comes next, with the
last of some farm buildings that stood at its southern end.

From Queen Street to Union Street

*

To the right is the house that formed the entrance to the Argyle Arcade, with, next to it,
a large malt barn that was taken down to be replaced by the buildings of Morrison's
Court. Near the barn is a mansion of the mercantile aristocracy built around 1775.
Next is the building that formed the southeast corner of Buchanan Street. Opposite it is
part of a small house, one half of which was removed to allow the formation of
Buchanan Street. Beside it is the mansion of John Gordon, a West India merchant. At

the narrow lane that is now Mitchell Street is an old thatched malt barn, the last to disappear of similar buildings at one time common along Argyle Street. On the opposite side of the lane are a few small houses and then the opening that is now Union Street.

From Union Street to Hope Street
*

This drawing continues the line from Union Street, the first buildings being workshops. The tall plain building that stood at the corner of Alston Street, formerly Playhouse Close, was Glasgow's first theatre, opened in 1764 by Mrs Bellamy, at which time those against theatricals set fire to the stage. The theatre was restored, but in April 1782 a second fire broke out that left no part of it standing except the blackened walls, which were used in constructing a granary, the upper part of which can be seen rising beyond some two-storey houses that front the street. Beside the trees on the left is a large brewing establishment demolished when Hope Street (then Copenhagen Street) was built. The whole area between Union Street and Hope Street was once the village of Grahamston, now entirely covered by Central Station.

While the most desirable residential address during the late eighteenth century was the relatively small New Town, its lifespan as a residential suburb was short. By the 1820s it had become commercialised. Warehouses and inns had taken over from housing and the wealthy had moved farther west to the new, most salubrious residential area in the city, Blythswood New Town, built on the former estate of Colin Campbell. The estate reached from the present-day West Nile Street to Pitt Street and from Argyle Street north to include Garnethill.

Bath Street (1800) was the first street to be opened in Blythswood. Gordon Street (1802), St Vincent Street (1804) and West Nile Street (1808) followed. Soon, other gridiron pattern streets such as Regent and Campberdown Place, now West George Street, crossed all sides of Blythswood Hill, which was crowned by Blythswood Square, the centre of Blythswood New Town. The square was originally called Garden Square after the developers, the Garden family. William Garden, who went bankrupt

View of Blythswood Place, St Vincent Street, 1828

in the attempt, started it in 1821. Other speculators took over from Garden, and architect John Brash laid the square out between 1823 and 1829. The houses on the west side of Blythswood Hill were built with their public rooms to the back to take advantage of the country view – old gardens, orchards and fields. Early buildings in Blythswood were stone-built classical terraces of two and three storeys with basements, many of which survive.

In the 1820s an even steeper hill than Blythswood was developed at Summerhill, now Garnethill. Sauchiehall Street, which, when a few villas with gardens were built on the north side, was straightened and widened about 1807, divided Blythswood and Garnethill. The widening of Sauchiehall Street extended only as far as Rose Street and did not reach Charing Cross until 1860. Charing Cross acquired its name only in 1855.

By the mid-1820s, Garden Street (now Bothwell Street), Waterloo Street, Cadogan Street and Holm Street had been created on the south part of the Blythswood estate. Land west of Jamaica Street had been built up with streets such as Oswald, Robertson, York, Brown and McAlpine. On the south side of the river, east and west of the ancient village of Gorbals, John and David Laurie had developed the areas of Tradeston, Hutcheston and Laurieston, the showpiece of which was the elegant riverside terraced Carlton Place, started in 1802.

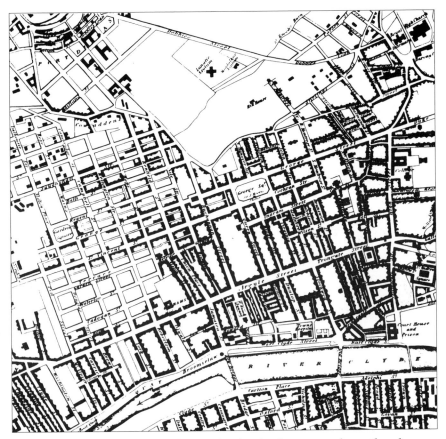

Map of Glasgow in the mid-1820s showing development on the north and south parts of the Blythswood estate. Note that Blythswood Square is called Garden Square, Sauchiehall Street is Saucheyhall and Argyle Street finished at Jamaica Street. Union Street is shown as Union Place. Also shown is the Royal Infirmary (1790s), the Trades House (1793) and the new Hutchesons' Hospital (1805).

By 1830 building operations nearly connected the villages of Calton, Anderston and Bridgeton, which, in 1846, were annexed to Glasgow.

MANSIONS

At the beginning of the eighteenth century Glasgow had few self-contained houses. Even people of rank and wealth lived in flats in the tenements around the Cross. Every room contained a bed, and the lady of the house would entertain visitors in her bedroom. Food was eaten in bedrooms, the house's

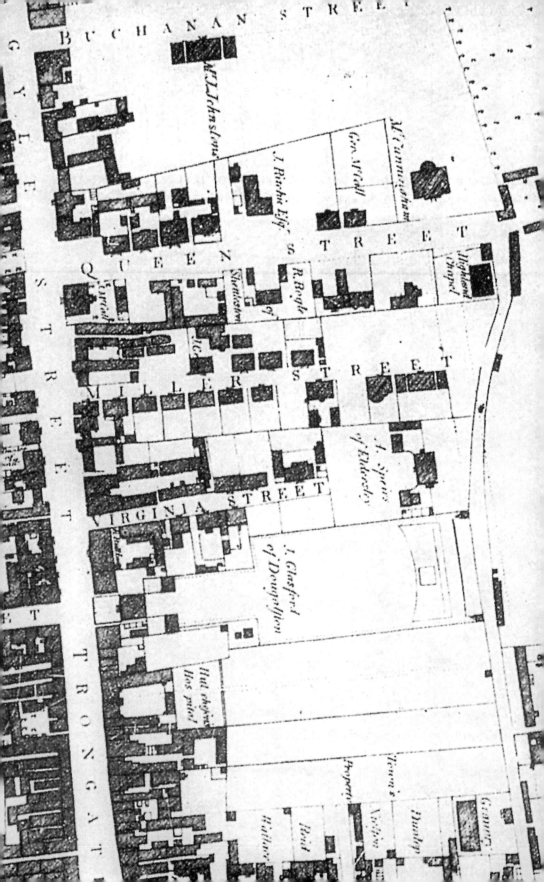

single public room being used only for special occasions. Because of the limited house accommodation, the better classes frequented taverns, and each evening gentlemen would adjourn to their clubs, which met there. Lawyers and doctors also met their clients in such establishments.

The tenement style of living continued until the 1750s when wealthy merchants began building mansions for themselves on land west of the city. John McArthur's *Plan of the City of Glasgow*, 1778, shows the location of the town houses of the leading merchants living in the Argyle Street/Trongate area. The houses were marked as those of 'J. Ritchie Esq., Mr Cunningham', 'A. Speirs of Ellersley', 'J Glasford of Dougalston', 'R. Bogle of Shettleston', and so on. Many were called by the names of their estates. At the time there was only one house in Buchanan Street, that of Mr J. Johnstone, which lay on the west side of the street. The only mansion remaining is the one that belonged to Mr Cunningham, which, with a portico added to the front and a large hall to the back, became the Royal Exchange in 1827. It now houses the Gallery of Modern Art.

THE SHAWFIELD MANSION

*

The first person to move out of the overcrowded medieval city into a detached mansion set amid gardens was Daniel Campbell of Shawfield. His house, built in 1712 on the north side of the Trongate just inside the West Port, was designed by lawyer turned architect Colin Campbell, who later found fame in England for his Palladian house designs and for publishing the foundation book of British eighteenth-century architecture, *Vitruvius Britannicus*. The Shawfield Mansion was an extremely early example of a Palladian villa in Britain. It had a pavilion-roofed seven-bay frontage with a pedimented three-bay projecting centrepiece. Two stone sphinxes graced the entrance.

Left.
John McArthur's Plan of the City of Glasgow, 1778, giving the location of the town houses of the leading merchants. The one marked as belonging to J. Glasford was the famous Shawfield Mansion and that belonging to A. Speirs was known as Virginia Mansion. The mansion at the corner of Argyle Street and Queen Street went by the name of 'McCall's Black House'. The stone for the house was taken from the 'Black Quarry' and, never having been painted, the building had an almost black appearance, hence the nickname. A very elegant house, it had a double stair in front and at least forty windows on four sides, making it extremely light and airy inside. As it was a corner house, the coach entrance and gardens were to the side. There was great sadness amongst the citizens of Glasgow when this fine old mansion was demolished.

Shawfield Mansion.

The house was the scene of rioting in June 1725, afterwards known as the 'Shawfield Riots'. At the time Daniel Campbell was the Member of Parliament for the Glasgow 'District of Burghs' and was unpopular for favouring the raising of tobacco tax. When he voted for an extension of the malt tax to Scotland that would put three old pence on each barrel of beer he became even more disliked. When it was rumoured that he had ordered the military into Glasgow on the first day of the malt tax, however, so inflamed were the citizens that to shouts of 'Down with Shawfield's House! No malt tax!' a mob, armed with hatchets, axes, knives and scythes, attacked and sacked his mansion. Campbell had wisely removed himself and his family to his country residence several days before the tax was to be enforced.

When the soldiers were called out they fired on the mob, killing nine people and wounding seventeen. A couple of weeks later, under a government warrant, nineteen citizens were arrested for 'encouraging and winking at the riot'. The provost and his magistrates were also arrested and imprisoned in Edinburgh Castle. Next day they were bailed and released.

On their release, the provost and magistrates wasted no time in getting on their horses and heading for Glasgow but, about six or seven miles outside the city, they were alarmed when they saw about two hundred horsemen riding towards them. On hearing the sound of cheering, however, they realised it was a welcome committee. The riders formed a guard of honour round the provost and the magistrates, and when the procession entered the city, the bells began to ring and thousands of citizens waved and cheered their civic heroes.

No action was taken against the provost and magistrates. The nineteen citizens arrested were not so lucky. Several were whipped through the streets and two were banished for life. Captain Bushell, who had given the order to fire on the mob, was put on trial but acquitted.

Campbell applied to the government for compensation and was awarded £6,080, a massive amount in 1725. With it he bought the island of Islay. Glasgow had to pay the compensation and, with other outlays, the riots cost the city almost £10,000, raised by a tax on the ale and beer sold in the town. Two years after the riots, Campbell sold the house to the West Indian merchant William McDowell.

The Shawfield Mansion had an illustrious visitor at the end of December 1745: Bonnie Prince Charlie. He had marched his beleaguered, bedraggled Highland army into Glasgow and decided that the most imposing house in the city was where he would reside. There he held court as best he could, as Glasgow, apart from a few Jacobite supporters, was hostile to the Jacobites.

Tobacco merchant John Glassford bought the house in 1760 and lived in it until his death in 1783. Nine years later his son sold the house to builder William Horn, who demolished it to lay out a new street through the site and that of the orchard and garden. The street was named Great Glassford Street, now just Glassford Street. John Glassford paid £1,785 for the house in 1760. His son sold it for £9,850. The sphinxes, part of the stone balustrade and some bits and pieces were all that were preserved of the city's most impressive eighteenth-century house.

THE VIRGINIA MANSION
*

Daniel Campbell set a fashion, and in 1756 Provost George Buchanan built his splendid Virginia Mansion on land he bought just west of the Shawfield Mansion. So that Buchanan could have an avenue leading to his house, he built it at the rear of the site instead of having it front the Trongate. With its classical seven-bay facade, the Virginia Mansion was very similar to the Shawfield Mansion. Inside it had a spacious square lobby with an inlaid

Virginia Mansion.

mosaic floor. The ceilings and walls of the ground-floor apartments were ornamented with plaster festoons of fruit and flowers, while the panelling had beautifully painted landscapes. Nothing obstructed the outlook in any direction. To the front was the River Clyde, to the back open fields. To the east were the Shawfield Gardens and those of Hutchesons' Hospital. To the west there was nothing as far as the eye could see. The mansion was totally out of town.

George Buchanan lived in the house until his death in 1769. As his son was a minor at the time, his trustees sold the house to his uncle, Alexander Speirs of Elderslie, in 1770.

Virginia Street had been laid out in 1753 and progressed northwards until it reached the Virginia Mansion that had been designed to close the street. In 1841, the Union Bank replaced the mansion and took over the role of closing the street.

THE DREGHORN MANSION

*

Not everyone built mansions to the west of Trongate. In 1752 Allan Dreghorn built his south of the Cross, in Great Clyde Street at the foot of Stockwell Street. Allan Dreghorn was the designer of St Andrew's Church and the first man in town to use a four-wheeled carriage. Like the Shawfield Mansion, the Dreghorn house was Palladian in design and was so exceptional that visitors to the city were taken to see it.

Dreghorn Mansion.

As Allan Dreghorn had no son, his nephew, Robert Dreghorn, inherited the mansion beside the river. When Robert also inherited the estate of Ruchill from his father, he was staggeringly wealthy, having an income of something like £8,000 a year, tremendous riches at that time. He was so ugly, however, that he was nicknamed 'Bob Dragon' and served as a 'bogie man' when mothers wanted to quieten their children. He had an aquiline nose that was turned considerably to one side of his face, was blind in one eye and squinted with the other. He was also horribly pockmarked. Nevertheless, his ugliness did not deter him from thinking he was God's gift to women. He greatly admired the fair sex and used to follow any good-looking female who took his fancy. When he caught up with the object of his attention, he would openly ogle her, upon which the girl usually started laughing. Unable to tolerate his sad life, Bob committed suicide in 1806 in the Dreghorn Mansion, said thereafter to be haunted.

For years the haunted house lay empty until, influenced by its low rent, oil and colour merchant George Provan occupied it as his home and place of business. On 17 February 1822 he had reason to regret his decision. Apparently a man had looked through a basement window and had seen what he thought were rivers of blood and the severed heads of two children. When word spread that Provan was a resurrectionist, a mob broke into his house and threw many of the contents into the river except, that is, those objects set aside to be taken away. The magistrates called out the military and the cavalry, and the infantry arrived in double quick time. The Riot Act was then read and the troops charged, upon which the mob fled.

Five people were arrested as being at the forefront of the sacking of the mansion. All were convicted and sentenced to transportation beyond the seas. Richard Campbell, an ex-police officer, was judged the ringleader and, besides transportation, was to be whipped through the city by the hangman, Thomas Young. This was done on 8 May and was the last whipping through Glasgow by the last Glasgow hangman. If the man who had looked through the basement window had had a closer look, he would have discovered the rivers of blood were red paint and there were no severed heads.

Flats now stand on the site of the unlucky Dreghorn Mansion.

The Crawford Mansion

*

Today's Queen Street Station is built on the site of the mansion built by Bailie George Crawford. Little is known about Crawford, but his house was well known, especially when owned by James Ewing, known as 'Craw' Ewing because of the many crows that nested in the tall trees surrounding his mansion. The garden, which had an oval lawn in front, was referred to as 'The Queen Street Park'. In 1838 Ewing sold his house and all his property in the vicinity to the Edinburgh and Glasgow Railway Company, which wanted the land in order to build a station on it. Glasgow's oldest station, Queen Street Station, or Dundas Street Station as it was first called, opened in 1842.

PUBLIC BUILDINGS

As well as housing and commercial premises, many fine public buildings were built in Glasgow between 1707 and 1837. Of these, only the following remain: St Andrew's Church (1793) in St Andrew's Square, Robert Adam's Trades House (1791) in Glassford Street, David Hamilton's Hutchesons'

Bailie Crawford's mansion in Queen Street.

Hospital (1802) in Hutcheson Street, William Stark's St George's Tron Church (1807) in Buchanan Street, William Stark's High Court (1809) in Saltmarket and St David's (Ramshorn Church) (1824) in Ingram Street.

TOWN HOSPITAL AND POORHOUSE
*

Glasgow's first major public building of the eighteenth century was the Town Hospital and Poorhouse, built by the Town Council, General Session, Trades House and Merchants House in 1733, on the old Green in Great Clyde Street at what is now the corner of Ropework Lane. The hospital was created to 'aliment and educate upwards of one hundred and fifty-two poor decayed old men, widows, and orphans of the city'. It was also hoped it would put an end to street begging. After the hospital was built, however, the population increased so much that it was decided to revive the old way of giving a badge to poor people born in Glasgow so that people knew they were not giving money to idlers or strangers.

The hospital originally comprised a front and wings but later a large detached building was erected in the back garden. The new building housed an infirmary with a lunatic asylum below, consisting of a few small cells that

Town Hospital and Poorhouse; painting by Thomas Fairbairn.

Opposite.
The Townhouse, Trongate, c. 1828; engraving by Joseph Swan.

were often flooded when the Clyde rose. Described as 'of modern fashion and so grand that nothing of that kind at Rome or Venice comes up to its magnificence', the hospital was much admired by strangers who thought it resembled a palace more than a poor house.

At first paupers were reticent to become inmates of the hospital, an institution comparatively new in Scotland at that time and associated in the minds of the poor with restrictions and deprivation. So, to encourage the destitute to live there, the directors declared that they would 'enjoy a desirable measure of liberty, good company, convenience for retirement, peace and quiet, freedom from all hurtful toil and care, with good provisions, liberty to go to church on the Sabbath and to week-day sermons and to see their friends, with abundant means of instruction and edification.' The declaration had the desired effect, for at the end of the first year there were 151 inmates, 61 old people and 90 children.

In 1844 the Town Hospital was closed, and a building in Parliamentary Road vacated by the Royal Lunatic Asylum when it moved to Gartnavel in 1843 was taken over as the City Poorhouse. The old Town Hospital was reopened during the cholera epidemic of 1848–49.

A warehouse replaced the Town Hospital.

THE TOWNHOUSE, TRONGATE

By the end of the first quarter of the eighteenth century the accommodation in the Tolbooth was cramped, and in 1735 the Council bought the land imme-diately to its west to build a new Town Hall, which opened in 1740.

Designed by Allan Dreghorn, the Town Hall was a cultured sign of Glasgow's growing prosperity. It was the city's most notable eighteenth-century structure, and no municipal building of its importance survives from then. Although said to be inspired by Inigo Jones and Isac de Caux's arcaded Covent Garden of 1631, the design of the new municipal seat echoed Glasgow's seventeenth-century arcaded buildings. The lower storey formed a broad piazza with five arches whose keystones were formed by a grotesque stone face. Between the windows of the two upper floors were fluted Ionic pilasters supporting a balustraded parapet topped with urns.

The spacious and elegant Town Hall, containing portraits of all the sovereigns of Great Britain starting with James VI, was on the first floor. The municipal chambers were on the second. In 1758–60 an identical further five bays were added to the west of the Town Hall, the keystones of the arches being carved with grotesque faces similar to those of the first five arches. The new portion of the building contained Assembly Rooms. Both the first half of the building and the second half had four shops on the ground floor under the piazza.

In 1781 the Tontine Society bought the whole building at the Cross that lay to the west of the old Tolbooth, with the exception of the Town Hall, with the intention of turning it into the Tontine Hotel and Coffee Room. Also planned was to add an extension to the back of the building of the same size and width as the front. The financing of the project was to be by a Tontine system whereby the surviving shareholder inherits the shares of all the subscribers who predecease him. There were 170 shares of £50. (The word 'Tontine' comes from Count Laurence Tonti, an Italian who first established such a society – a cross between a lottery and life assurance.) The Council stipulated that the Tontine Society was to keep the Assembly Rooms open until new ones could be built. This was agreed, and all the public functions and dances were held there until the new Assembly Rooms were built in Ingram Street in 1796.

The Coffee Room on the ground floor was opened on 4 May 1784 with the most splendid ball ever seen in Glasgow, 'at which no distinction of ranks was regarded'. It was recorded that the room was so densely crowded that there was scarcely room for dancing.

Entered from the piazza, widened from 11 feet to 27 feet, the Coffee Room, or Exchange as it became, on the ground floor was 74 feet by 32 feet 6 inches and over 16 feet high. It was an elegantly decorated oval room partly lit by a glass dome supported by Doric columns and was 'universally allowed to be the most elegant of its kind in Britain if not in Europe'. For a subscription of around 25 shillings, members had access to Scottish, English, Irish and Continental newspapers and reviews, magazines and other periodical publications. Strangers were admitted free of charge and for a limited time were allowed all the privileges of subscribers, 'a liberality it was believed, not equalled in any other great town in the island'.

Just as the coffee house of Lloyds was the commercial centre of London, the Tontine Coffee House was the commercial centre of Glasgow. When the driver of the mail coach had important news to deliver, he would gallop his horses along the Gallowgate, sounding his bugle as a signal that he had such a dispatch. It was within the walls of the old Coffee House, therefore, that the news of great events like Nelson's victory at Trafalgar and Wellington's victory at Waterloo were first made known to the citizens of Glasgow.

The hotel was often referred to as 'The Tontine Hottle' as it was the first of its kind in Glasgow and the citizens were unused to the word 'hotel'.

Although the Council had moved its administration away from the Cross in 1814, the Town Hall, then known as the Tontine Hall, remained as a public hall until 1854 when its swan song was a banquet on the official unveiling of the equestrian statue of Queen Victoria, now in George Square.

In 1867 the Improvement Trustees bought the Hotel and converted it into a shop which drapers Moore Taggart & Co. occupied. The famous piazzas were filled in at that time. In 1911, the building was so badly damaged by fire that it had to be demolished. Today's red sandstone warehouse and office block replaced Glasgow's finest eighteenth-century civic building. The name Tontine lives on in the lane alongside the red sandstone building, and some of the famous Tontine heads are now in the garden behind Provand's Lordship.

THE THEATRE ROYAL,
QUEEN STREET
*

Although dancing featured prominently in the social life of Glasgow, theatre-going did not, as after the Reformation plays and theatrical performances of any kind were prohibited and denounced by ministers from their pulpits. Only the more enlightened were devotees of the play. There is a much repeated story that Glasgow's first theatre, a wooden lean-to built in 1752 against a ruined wall of the Bishop's Castle, was burned down by religious fanatics incited by the Reverend George Whitefield who denounced it as a house of the devil. According to Whitefield, what happened was that the theatre's manager removed the building's roof when the players had finished.

Because of the opposition of citizens and the authorities, the city's first permanent theatre was built in 1762 outside the city boundary in the suburb of Grahamston, the nearest village to the west. It opened in 1764, when an attempt was made to set it on fire. Drama was still regarded as a form of devil worship by the poorer people and the authorities. Fire did eventually destroy the theatre and arson was suspected. Nevertheless, attitudes began to change, especially among the educated, and eventually the Glasgow magistrates gave permission for a theatre to be built within the city. The Theatre Royal opened in Dunlop Street in 1782, but by the end of the century was so inadequate that a new Theatre Royal was built in 1803 at the corner of Queen Street.

The new theatre, which cost £18,500, mostly raised by public subscription, was described as being 'the most magnificent provincial theatre in the Empire' when it opened on 24 April 1805. Designed by David Hamilton, the

Joseph Swan's view of the Theatre Royal with the Royal Bank to its left.

Adam-style building was three storeys high with five doorways, the centre three leading to the two tiers of boxes, those to the north and south to the pit and the two galleries. Above the doorways were six 30-foot-high Ionic pillars supporting a rich entablature.

While the outside of the building was rather heavy and gloomy, the interior was elegant and elaborately decorated. It had a proscenium 30 feet wide and a stage large enough to represent any scenic exhibition. Edinburgh portrait artist Alexander Naismith designed the striking scenery, which included a famous drop scene of the Firth of Clyde. The theatre seated 1,500 people, was open four nights a week and had takings of £250 a night. There were two seasons: Winter, from November to January, and Summer, April until July.

Although many great acts appeared in the Queen Street theatre, the advertised appearance of the great tragedian Edmund Kean created a commotion. Not only townspeople but also those from farther afield were desperate to attend the performance. For weeks the theatre had been fully booked and temporary boxes were erected on the stage. People besieged the theatre's doors for hours before they were due to open, and when they did, the tremendous surge resulted in many having their clothes torn and others

Ruins of Theatre Royal, Queen Street.

their pockets picked. Men fought and women fainted and had to be taken into the theatre, as it was impossible to get them out because of the crowds pushing in. The performance did not live up to expectation, however, and by the fifth act nothing could be heard from the stage for the hisses, boos and groans from the audience who had begun to leave in disgust. The *Glasgow Herald* of 16 April 1817 reported that the general opinion was 'that Mr Kean was labouring under the effects of intoxication'.

There was only one other time when the audience equalled that of the appearance of Kean. It was on 18 September 1818, when crowds came to see the auditorium 'illuminated with Sparkling Gas'. According to advertisements 'the grand crystal lustre on the roof of the Queen Street house, the largest in Scotland, would, in place of wicks and candles and oil lamps, be illuminated with sparkling gas'. It was to be the first theatre in Britain to be so lit. A writer then said the effect on the audience when the gas was turned on was such as to leave 'some of them to fancy that they had been ushered into a new world'.

Despite the theatre having been built by public subscription, drama was not well supported in the city and successive managers struggled to make the theatre pay. Even the novelty of gas lighting did not help, and when on 10

The Grammar School, 204 George Street.

January 1829 the building burned down during a morning rehearsal, bad maintenance and open gas flames were blamed for the fire. Only part of the facade was left standing and as the management did not have insurance, the ruins were demolished.

THE GRAMMAR SCHOOL, 204 GEORGE STREET

*

In 1782 it was decided to build a new grammar school, the old sixteenth-century building having become unsuitable. A site was to be looked for that would be large enough to allow room for a playground, and in 1787 a plot on the north side of George Street was agreed on.

John Craig was the architect chosen to build the new school and the design he came up with was in the popular Adam style. The main frontage was of two storeys with slightly projecting wings of three storeys on each side. There was a ground-floor common hall in the central part of the building and six classrooms in each of the wings. The school moved into its new home in 1788. Before long the accommodation was inadequate, however, and when the roll had reached 580 in 1820 a site for a new school was found just behind the George Street one. The school moved there in 1821 and the George Street building was advertised for sale. It was described as being light and cheerful in appearance, with two staircases and six large halls, each having two fireplaces, six windows and four ventilators.

The Andersonian College moved into the George Street building, added to it and remodelled it, the classical pedimented porch being from this period. Over the years the College amalgamated with other institutions, and in 1886 it became the Glasgow and West of Scotland Technical College (Royal from 1912). At the beginning of the twentieth century, the College decided to demolish the old Grammar School building and replace it with David Barclay's giant red stone Italianate College of 1901–09. Strathclyde University evolved from the Andersonian College.

HUNTERIAN MUSEUM, OLD COLLEGE GROUNDS

*

William Hunter, the famous surgeon and anatomist who was born at East Kilbride in 1718 and educated at Glasgow University, founded the Hunterian Museum, Glasgow's first museum. Hunter went to London where, amongst other important posts, he was physician to the Queen and President of the Royal College of Physicians. When he died in 1783, Hunter bequeathed his collections, accumulated over half a century, to his old university along with £8,000 to build a museum to house the objects, valued at over £100,000. The collections included zoological and mineral specimens, a library of over 12,000 books, manuscripts, coins, medals, paintings, archaeological artefacts and anatomical and pathological specimens relating to Hunter's work. Among the paintings were works by Murillo, Guido, Titian, Rembrandt, Rubens and Sir Joshua Reynolds.

Architect William Stark was commissioned to design the Museum, which was to stand at the west end of the Old College Garden. The front formed a Roman-Doric portico of six columns rising from a flight of steps behind which was a recess and a second row of columns. The columns supported an ornamented pediment. Behind the massive front rose a stone dome surmounted by a glass cupola that gave a graceful finish to the building, which some considered to be the finest of the period in Britain. The simplicity of the exterior was echoed in the interior, which had a central circular hall with rooms around it. The saloon for paintings was particularly beautifully proportioned and decorated. The Museum opened to the public on 26 August 1808 and was demolished around 1885 with the rest of the University buildings.

Hunterian Museum from the west,
drawn by J. Fleming and engraved by Joseph Swan.

LUNATIC ASYLUM,
PARLIAMENTARY ROAD

*

William Stark's last work in Glasgow was the Lunatic Asylum in Parliamentary Road, begun in 1810 and opened in 1814. Stark died prematurely in 1813 at the age of forty-three.

By the beginning of the nineteenth century, it was recognised that the cells housing lunatics in the Town Hospital were unsuitable for their purpose. It was therefore decided to build in Bell's Park the city's first lunatic asylum, the intention being 'to restore the use of reason, to alleviate suffering, and lessen peril, where reason cannot be restored'.

Before designing the Glasgow Asylum, Stark, along with members of the proposed Asylum's General Committee, visited a number of recent asylums in Britain. By the end of the tour, Stark had firm ideas on how the constituent parts of the Glasgow Asylum should be arranged. On working out his plan for the Asylum, Stark defined four categories of severity of illness or 'degrees of

View of William Stark's Lunatic Asylum from Bell's Park,
engraved by Joseph Swan.

insanity' – 'Frantic', 'Incurable', 'Ordinary' and 'Convalescent'. He then divided the building according to these categories. Based on a saltire plan, the centre was an octagon from which radiated four oblong ward wings, three storeys in height. The wings allowed for the patients to be divided according to sex, rank in life and degree of insanity. A similar arrangement applied in the spacious exercise grounds consisting of gravel walks, flower plots and shrubbery. Each ward had a long, narrow gallery in which the patients took exercise in bad weather. To prevent one category of patient being disturbed by even a glance from a patient of any other category, bedroom windows were placed high in the wall.

The octagonal centre of the building had a massive open staircase and a circular attic storey. From the attic rose a smaller octagon that housed a chapel surmounted by a great dome, mainly of glass, supported on internal columns. The dome, as one writer put it, 'would always remain one of the greatest ornaments of the city'. Eight large windows in the side of the dome lit the chapel and the staircase.

William Adam's University Library (left) and east side of the Hamilton Building (right). The ugly outside staircase added to the Library not long before the University moved to Gilmorehill is clearly seen.

Stark's Asylum was built to accommodate 100 patients, with 136 apartments for them. Four large and two small furnaces provided heating, hot air passing through the building by means of a vent system. Patients had to pay for their keep according to a sliding scale rising from eight shillings a week for paupers to three guineas for an upper-class patient. For the latter, the eating rooms, parlours and bedrooms were spacious and genteelly furnished. Often the upper-class apartments consisted of a suite of rooms to allow personal servants to wait on the patients.

Despite extensions, the Asylum was considered old-fashioned by 1841 and plans were drawn up for a new institution at Gartnavel. When Gartnavel opened in 1843, Stark's building was taken over as the City Poorhouse, which it remained until its demolition in 1908.

Stark's Glasgow Lunatic Asylum was considered an achievement of genius, an architectural masterpiece, and was thought to be the only building of that form in Britain. Despite the country views and the spaciousness of the building and grounds, however, it was a 'total' institution, isolating inmates not only from each other but also from the outside world.

THE LOST FAMILY – THE ADAMS IN GLASGOW

For a city that could destroy a medieval castle and mutilate a medieval cathedral, it is not surprising that it would demolish buildings designed by the great family of architects, the Adams, who founded a style of architecture that was marked by a fine sense of proportion and an elegant taste in classical decoration. Edinburgh preserved its Adams buildings; Glasgow destroyed them, except for the Trades House in Glassford Street and Pollok House. The blame for Glasgow's barbarous treatment of its Adams buildings rests not only on the shoulders of Victorian and Edwardian Philistines but also on those of the twentieth century. The Adams buildings Glasgow wantonly destroyed are: the Old College Library, Kelvingrove House, the Assembly Rooms, the Royal Infirmary, two tenements in High Street and David Dale's mansion.

THE OLD COLLEGE LIBRARY

*

William Adam's Library was built between 1732 and 1744 in the grounds of the Old College behind the main buildings and northeast of Blackfriars Church. It was a handsome building with a decorative pediment and Corinthian pilasters. In 1775, a visitor described it as 'a very noble room with a gallery round it supported by pillars'. An ugly outside staircase was added a few years before the University moved to Gilmorehill in the 1880s. When first built, the Library stood alone but later appeared to be tacked on to the Hamilton Building, completed in 1811. The Hamilton Building, which provided extra classrooms and a new common hall, replaced the whole eastern part of the inner quadrangle and required the removal of the old northeast and southeast corner turrets. The Hunterian Museum also overshadowed the Library. As had happened so often, with no regard for its heritage, Glasgow demolished the gem of a Library along with the rest of the College. It could easily have been moved elsewhere as it was not large. William was the father of Robert and James Adam, the two celebrated architect brothers.

KELVINGROVE HOUSE

*

In 1782, Patrick Colquhoun was elected Lord Provost of Glasgow at the age of thirty-seven. The same year he bought twelve acres of ground on the banks of the River Kelvin, west of the city, and commissioned Robert Adam to design a mansion for him. When Colquhoun's country house was finished, he called it Kelvingrove, the name still used for the park.

Colquhoun was the instigator and first President of Glasgow Chamber of Commerce, and while he seemed set for a brilliant career in Glasgow, in 1789 he left the city, going first to Ostend and Bruges, where he acted as agent for the Chamber, and finally to London, where he reorganised the police force. He returned to Glasgow only once, in 1797, to receive an LLD from the University.

Although the exterior of Kelvingrove House was said to combine the elements of late Roman classicism in an original 'almost whimsical way', the interior had the typical delicate plasterwork and attractive fireplaces associated with Adam. An advertisement of 1790 assures us it had a bath, possibly the city's first. The River Kelvin supplied the water.

In 1792 Colquhoun sold his property to John Pattison, who added about twelve acres to it. After a couple of ownership changes, enthusiastic archer Robert Knox rented the house and often held archery competitions in the grounds. There are pictures in Glasgow Art Gallery showing the competitions. In 1854 Glasgow Corporation purchased the estate and added largely to it to form Kelvingrove Park.

In 1871 the Corporation turned the mansion into the city's first museum and art gallery, which became so popular with the public that in 1874 John Carrick, the City Architect, designed an extension so large that it dwarfed Colquhoun's fine old mansion, a wing of which was demolished to make room for the extension. Although the museum's main exhibits related to all aspects of Glasgow's industries, it had a large collection of natural history and miscellaneous objects. There was also an aquarium containing Scottish freshwater fish. Exhibited outside the building was an antique steam engine apparently constructed for James Watt.

During preparations for the 1901 Exhibition, to clear space for an Exhibition Concert Hall, it was proposed to demolish Kelvingrove House, one of Robert Adam's most original designs. There was a public outcry, but, as usual in Glasgow, that meant nothing to the authorities. To add insult to injury, John Carrick's extension was reprieved and, with a coat of white paint, became the Exhibition's Japan Pavilion. The demolishment of a Georgian

*Kelvingrove House, photographed by Thomas Annan before it
was extended and turned into a museum and art gallery.*

mansion, especially an Adam one, against the wishes of the citizens was an
act of vandalism that had become characteristic of Glasgow.

GLASGOW ROYAL INFIRMARY
✳

Robert and James Adam designed Glasgow's first Royal Infirmary in 1792. (A
royal charter in 1791 incorporated the title 'Glasgow Royal Infirmary'.) The
site chosen for the Infirmary was the land on which the ruins of the Bishop's
Castle stood. Before the ruins could be cleared and building could begin,
however, a royal charter had to be obtained to grant the land, as it was
Crown property. Many of the stones of the old Castle were used in the new
building, the biggest contract the Adam brothers carried out in Glasgow.
Robert Adam died in 1792 before the work was completed. His brother died
two years later. The south wing of its successor today occupies the site of the
building.

The general form of the building was a parallelogram with bold projec-

The Royal Infirmary.

tions in the centre and wings. It had four storeys above ground and a basement. The front part of the central basement, the main entrance to the building, supported four Corinthian columns, two of which stood on each side of a Venetian window. Behind the columns, the wall was ornamented with pilasters with a pediment above. The wings had giant Venetian windows, two storeys high, with semi-circular windows in the basement. In the basement were cells for the temporary confinement of the insane, baths, one hot and one cold, an apothecary's shop, the kitchen and other apartments. Crowning the whole structure was a light and graceful dome, glazed between the ribs, which rested on a sculpted circular base. Under the dome was a spacious circular operating room. Although most considered the building to be a structure of much beauty and elegance and a chief ornament of the city, some held that its claims on public admiration were overrated and that 'the whole composition wanted breadth'. You can never please everyone.

When the hospital opened in December 1794 there were eight wards, each with seventeen beds, making 136 beds in all. Although in 1798, in an

Right.
Close-up of centre Venetian window with its four Corinthian
columns topped by a pediment.

attempt to halt epidemics, thousands of people were vaccinated free of charge with Edward Jenner's cowpox vaccine, by 1799, only five years after the opening, 14 per cent of the admissions suffered from fever. By 1828 the figure was 40 per cent, and by 1837 almost 75 per cent of those admitted were fever cases. Out of 7,200 treated in 1837, 5,387 had fever. To cope with continued epidemics, a new wing was built in 1816 and a fever block was added in 1829. In 1861, a new surgical block was opened, bringing the total number of beds to 572.

By the end of the nineteenth century other blocks had been added to the Infirmary, and in 1897 it was decided that a modern building should replace the front block, the Adam building, which, despite the basement being converted to a full ground floor in 1850 and the addition of low wings, was substantially intact. A great deal of controversy surrounded the decision to demolish the historic building, but no notice was taken and the first Royal Infirmary was taken down in 1912. Glasgow had lost another Adam building. It is beyond understanding how supposedly educated people could demolish a building designed by the Adam brothers whose work was renowned world-wide. None but a Glasgow worthy would have considered destroying such an architectural gem.

In 1924, despite pleas and fierce objections from medical councils at home and abroad to preserve it, the Infirmary managers decided that the Lister Ward, famous for its connection with Joseph Lister, who pioneered the use of antisepsis in surgery while working at the Royal Infirmary, should be pulled down. There is a reconstruction of the ward in the Wellcome Medical Museum in London. The Royal Faculty of Physicians and Surgeons in Glasgow was gifted the fireplace from the ward and a table.

ASSEMBLY ROOMS, INGRAM STREET

✳

When the Tontine Assembly Rooms became too small to accommodate the social activities of the city, new Rooms were built farther west, in Ingram Street. They were designed by Robert and James Adam and were paid for by Tontine shares of £10 each. Although the foundation stone was laid on 11 March 1792, work did not begin until 1796, by which time the Adam brothers were dead. At ground level, the facade of the two-storey building was rusticated, with a square, bold projection in the centre that supported four handsome Ionic columns, two on each side of a large, elegant Venetian window.

Joseph Swan's engraving of the Assembly Rooms.

Behind the columns were pilasters. There was also a pilastered Venetian window on either side of the centre projection. Topping the whole was a balustraded entablature. The proportions and detailing of the building were exceptionally fine.

The principal room, lit by the Venetian windows, was 80 feet by 35 feet and 27 feet high. This elegantly decorated hall, in which 'the beauty and fashion of the west were wont to trip on the light fantastic toe', was reached from the entrance hall by a hanging stair. Apart from the hall, used for concerts, public dinners and assemblies, there were card, supper and retiring rooms. Two wings harmonising with the original building were added in 1807.

Attractions in the Assembly Rooms were diverse, from 'Grand Concerts' by Chopin to an exhibition advertised as 'Napoleon Breathing – the most wonderful anatomical figure in the world composed of a new and artificial substance termed "Sarkomos"'. It represents Napoleon reposing on a couch clad in military costume with his *own hat and sword* and is 'universally allowed to be the most perfect artificial figure ever brought before the public'. Admittance was one shilling, children sixpence.

When the building was demolished in the 1890s to make way for an extension to the Post Office, part of it was saved. At his own expense, Bailie James McLennan removed the arch forming the facade's centrepiece and had it rebuilt as a triumphal arch at the east end of London Road. After another move, it finished up in its present position near the Saltmarket entrance to Glasgow Green. The semi-circular carriage archway was once the central window of the facade. Between the columns are pedestrian openings. The impressive gateway serves as a monument to at least one official of Glasgow Corporation being cultured enough to recognise that an Adam building should not have been demolished. Astonishingly, the 1907 wings added to the Assembly Rooms survived until 1911.

Our Victorian and early twentieth-century forebears demolished all the Adam buildings mentioned so far, but the next two Adam buildings, David Dale's mansion in Charlotte Street and College Buildings in High Street, were demolished in the 1950s and 1970s when our city fathers should have been more enlightened. (Glasgow has only now learned from its mistakes.) William Morris said that 'old buildings are not in any sense our property to do as we like with them. We are only trustees for those that come after us.' What a pity that Glasgow's past civic leaders never believed likewise – irreplaceable architectural gems would not have been lost.

DAVID DALE'S HOUSE, CHARLOTTE STREET

*

Although, to many, the name David Dale means nothing, he was a citizen of Glasgow worthy of remembrance on many counts but particularly as 'the father of the cotton trade in Scotland'. He was born in Stewarton in 1739 and after a weaving apprenticeship began dealing in linen by tramping the country with a pack. Moving to Glasgow in 1763, he set up a yarn-importing business in a small shop at the foot of High Street. Sensing, however, that manufacturing offered greater opportunities, he bought machinery and began weaving linen cloths. His business thrived, and by 1783 he had opened the first branch of the Royal Bank in Glasgow, was a founder member of the Chamber of Commerce and a magistrate. What brought him to the attention of a wider public, however, was the founding, with Richard Arkwright, of the New Lanark cotton mills (1786), the first of any importance in Scotland. They

Right.
View of David Dale's mansion from the garden.

James Adam's tenements at 169–177 and 179–185 High Street around the beginning of the twentieth century before they were too neglected.

were not run like any others for, under the management of Dale's son-in-law, Robert Owen, they had the best working and living conditions in Britain. Dale had other mills but it is for those at New Lanark that he is best remembered.

David Dale strived to help people less fortunate than himself. Outside business, he was a zealous friend and helper 'in every good word and work'. He gave generously to many public institutions, among them the Royal Infirmary and Missionary and Bible Societies.

Originally a member of the Church of Scotland, Dale left it to help found a Congregational church. For thirty-seven years he preached in a church in Greyfriars Wynd built by his friend and fellow-philanthropist Archibald Paterson, who made his money in the candle trade. For obvious reasons, the church was commonly called the Caun'le Kirk.

Although religious, Dale was no sour, gloomy zealot. He was genial and humorous and enjoyed hospitality, as his corpulence proved. That he was short made him look even more rotund, and it is believed that his portly figure with cocked hat and cane was the inspiration for Sir Walter Scott's Baillie Nicol Jarvie in *Rob Roy*.

Not everyone agrees that when Dale and Paterson laid out Charlotte Street in 1779, Dale commissioned Robert Adam to design the houses, which were elegant mansions each with its own coach house. Most, however, agree that Dale's own house, the largest in the street, built in 1783 at the southwest corner adjacent to Glasgow Green, was the work of Adam. The house had two storeys at the front and four at the back, which included a basement and an attic. On the two main floors were four public rooms facing the street – a dining room, library and two drawing-rooms. Dale's study was an octagonal room on the second floor. Each room had a fireplace, even the wine cellar.

Dale's mansion remained in the family until 1827 when it was sold to Mr Moses McCulloch. By 1852, it had become the city's Eye Infirmary, with oculist Dr William McKenzie carrying out operations in Dale's octagonal study. Despite vigorous resistance, the house was demolished in 1954 to make way for an extension (never built) to Our Lady and St Francis' School. Glasgow had not learned any lessons from the past and another Adam building became rubble.

COLLEGE BUILDINGS, HIGH STREET

*

Amazingly, as late as the 1970s two A-listed tenements at the corners of College Street and High Street designed by James Adam in 1793 were unashamedly destroyed.

The buildings were the first phase of a development scheme by the University. Included in the scheme was a domed building that was never built. Although most architectural books say that the buildings were intended as University staff housing, apparently they were just a speculative venture by the University. Each building had three and a half storeys, the two principal floors being contained within a giant Corinthian order that included the Prince of Wales' feathers. Above the main cornice, the attic storey had square windows, some of which were flanked with circular medallions. The flats were large, with six or seven apartments. The southern tenement was altered in the nineteenth century when Ingram Street was extended to meet High Street.

For many years James Adam's fine buildings were neglected and later were threatened with removal to accommodate a new ring road. When the announcement did come that the buildings were to be demolished, there was an outcry from organisations such as the Institute of Architects. Their intervention was useless, and the buildings were destroyed in 1974 on the pretext that they were unsafe. How convenient!

HOTELS

A statute declared by King James I, on returning from captivity in England in 1442, was that 'hostels or public inns were to be provided for the accommodation of travellers'. In Glasgow, the earliest record of an inn is that of the Dove Inn (1595) which stood on the west side of High Street (covered in Chapter 2). Another inn already considered was the Burnt Barns, built in 1679. About the middle of the eighteenth century, the White Hart Inn, with stables, etc, stood at the Gallowgate corner of Ross Street. Behind the inn was a bowling green and garden. Its first landlord was Robert Tennent, who in 1754 built the first custom-made inn, the famous Saracen's Head in the Gallowgate. As already explained, the first time the word 'hotel' was used in Glasgow was when the Tontine Hotel opened.

SARACEN'S HEAD INN, GALLOWGATE

*

Although by the beginning of the second half of the eighteenth century there were quite a few inns in the city, the magistrates decided that none met the requirements of such an important city. On 24 November 1754, therefore, they sold the land of the kirkyard of Little St Mungo on the north side of Gallowgate to Robert Tennent, the owner of the nearby White Hart Inn, with the proviso that he should erect a first-class inn on the site according to an agreed plan. The old East Port adjoining the kirkyard had been removed in 1749 and permission was granted for the stones from this to be used in building the new inn, not stones from the Bishop's Palace as is often stated.

The inn was finished by 1755 and named the Saracen's Head, about which there is some mystery. One explanation is that it was taken from the name of a twelfth-century London inn once patronised by Richard the Lionheart on his return from a crusade. The inn's sign showed a man as large

The Old Saracen's Head Inn, north side of Gallowgate, in 1845 by which time it had
been added to and converted into houses and shops. As the illustration shows,
a library occupied part of the ground-floor premises.

as life down to the knees, dressed in a white turban and claret-coloured robe.
He had glaring eyes and a most alarming expression and was in the act of
drawing a scimitar out of its scabbard. He was meant to represent a Saracen.

Built of good hewn stone, the Saracen's Head Inn had a 100-foot
frontage, a recessed central portion and slightly protruding wings. Behind
was a ballroom with space for a hundred dancers or a large dinner party. Also
behind was a large court of offices and stables for sixty horses. The carriageway to the ballroom opened along the west side of the inn and was the origin
of the lane now known as the Great Dowhill; the entrance to the stables, a
private lane skirting the east side of the inn, became Saracen Lane. There was
a pump well in the yard, and it was thought to be a well created for the use
of the Chapel of Little Saint Mungo when it was founded in 1500, which,
considering the inn was built on the site of the chapel, was a reasonable
assumption. A central broad flight of steps led to the inn's entrance hall.

The advertisement in the *Glasgow Courant* of October 1755 intimating
the completion of Tennent's inn gave the following details:

Robert Tennent . . . takes this opportunity to acquaint all ladies
and gentlemen that at the desire of the magistrates of Glasgow,

he has built a convenient and handsome new inn, agreeable to a plan given him containing 36 fire-rooms now fit to receive lodgers. The bed chambers are all separate, none of them entering through another. . . . The beds are all very good, clean and free from bugs . . .

Building the inn bankrupted Tennent, who died less than two years after it opened. His creditors leased the inn to his widow for twelve years. When Tennent's widow died, the inn's next lessee was James Graham. When he died, *his* widow took over and under her regime the inn enjoyed its heyday of prosperity. She had to give it up when her second husband, James Buchanan, became bankrupt.

When on circuit the Lords of Justiciary would lodge at the inn where in the evening they would dine with the bailies (municipal magistrates), the joint being 'poor man', i.e. a shoulder blade of mutton accompanied by oceans of claret. In 1774 Dr Samuel Johnson and Boswell lodged at the inn on returning from their Hebridean tour. When the first mail coach to arrive in Glasgow from London drew up at the Saracen's Head in July 1788, two waiters dressed in embroidered coats, red plush knee breeches, silk stockings and powdered hair met it. According to *Jones' Directory* for 1789, the diligence for Edinburgh started at nine o'clock in the morning, 'or at any other hour that the first two passengers might agree on', and that for Ayr at 10 o'clock forenoon – both from 'James Buchanan's Saracen's Head'.

In 1791 William Miller of Slatefield purchased the building and converted it into shops and houses. He also built an addition to the east. For about fifty years the great ballroom was used as a place of worship by various sects, after which it became a reading school.

In 1904 the old inn was demolished and replaced by a tenement that has also been demolished except for the shops at ground level. Evidence that the site was once a burial ground was found when, during demolition, human bones were found in what were the inn's cellars. Human bones had also been found during the conversion to shops and houses in 1791. The Saracen's Head name lives on in a pub (referred to locally as the 'Sarry Heid') slightly east of the site of the old inn. There is a relic of the inn in the People's Palace, a blue and white giant punch bowl with a capacity of five gallons. It graced the head of the table on important occasions and was made in the Delftfield Pottery, situated on the north bank of the River Clyde near the Broomielaw Quay. The bowl bears all the marks of having been well used and has the inscription 'Success to the town of Glascow'.

BLACK BULL INN,
ARGYLE STREET

*

When the West Port was removed in 1751, buildings began to appear along the Westergate (later Argyle Street). One was a rival to the Saracen's Head – the Black Bull Inn at the corner of Argyle Street and Virginia Street, which opened in 1758. It was built by the Highland Society, formed in 1727 by seventeen gentlemen, originally from the Highlands, who had settled in Glasgow. The objective of the Society was to help poor Highlanders in the city. The money to build the inn mainly came from a generous collection taken after the Reverend George Whitefield preached a sermon in the Cathedral churchyard on behalf of the Society. The inn provided the Society's main source of income.

James Graham, the first landlord of the Black Bull, had been in charge of a similarly named inn across the road. The new inn, commonly known as the Highland Society's House, had twenty-nine bedrooms, a large dining room, a coffee room, a ballroom, nine parlours and stabling for thirty-eight horses. Its opening advertisement stated that 'great care has been taken to keep the bedrooms at a distance from the drinking rooms'.

Ironically, in May 1761 the body of Archibald, third Duke of Argyll, after whom Argyle Street had shortly before been named, lay in state in the Black Bull Hotel en route to the family vault at Kilmun. No one bothered much about spelling in those days, hence the reason for the different versions of 'Argyll'. When the Saracen's Head Inn closed, the Lords of Justiciary trans-ferred their patronage to its west end rival, the Black Bull. Dressed in their judicial robes, their Lordships would walk from the inn along Trongate to the old court at the Cross and, after 1812, down Saltmarket to the new court. The inn was much used by farmers and drovers, most of whom were Highland. Robert Burns stayed at the inn in 1787 and 1788, and from there penned some of his love letters to 'Clarinda', Mrs Agnes MacLehose. Marks & Spencer's store occupies the site of the Black Bull and a plaque on the Virginia Street corner commemorates Burns' connection with the inn.

The Black Bull was the headquarters of the Whig Club and a popular venue for hunt balls. Its courtyard was an ideal arena for settling all 'affairs of honour' among boys, as it had a pump well for washing the bloody noses. Seldom a day passed without two or three battles taking place there.

THE BUCK'S HEAD INN, ARGYLE STREET

✳

The Buck's Head Inn was originally one of the first two mansions erected in Argyle Street. Built in 1751, it belonged to Provost Murdoch. Alongside stood the companion house, built by Colin Dunlop. Murdoch's mansion was converted in 1790 into the Buck's Head Inn. The landlord was Peter Jardine, who married a widow whose dashing daughter was the first to drive a two-horsed phaeton in the city. The sign of the inn was a gilt stag's head. In 1820, when a radical rising was feared, the magistrates occupied the inn and remained alert night and day to deal with any emergency. It was also the headquarters of the officers of the 7th and 10th Hussars. Among famous guests who stayed at the inn were Sir Walter Scott, Thomas Telford and the Poet Laureate, Robert Southey, who was not impressed with its hospitality. 'We drove to the Buck's Head in Argyle Street. Large as the house is, they had no room with a fire, when we arrived cold and hungry at ten o'clock on a wet morning. The inns in large cities are generally detestable, and this does not appear to form an exception from the common rule.' The inn closed about 1860, and Alexander 'Greek' Thomson erected his Buck's Head warehouse on

Thomas Fairbairn's painting of the Buck's Head Inn with, on its left,
Colin Dunlop's mansion house, both built in 1751. When the painting was made,
the inn was still in use.

the site. The Buck's Head companion, Colin Dunlop's mansion, remained until 1922 when a clothing shop and a picture house replaced it, both now no more.

OTHER ESTABLISHMENTS
*

Among other inns in the city was the Eagle in Maxwell Street, a favourite resort of the nobility and gentry. A much talked about event once took place in its courtyard, a cockfight with 1,000 guineas as stakes. The participants were Provost Jacob Dixon of Dumbarton and Maule of Panmure, a notorious drinker and gambler. Dixon's bird won. There was also the Star Inn on the north side of Ingram Street, facing Glassford Street. It was in the Star that a reform association, 'The Friends of the Constitution and of the People', was formed. The Italian Centre now occupies the site. There were two popular inns in the Gallowgate, the Avondale, which had a notice 'Two noddies

*This photograph of the west side of George Square and St Vincent Place shows the
Waverly, Crow and Clarence Hotels shortly before the demolition of the first two
to make way for the headquarters of the Bank of Scotland in the late 1860s.
All the buildings in the photograph were replaced between the 1850s and 1906,
and it has to be said that the replacements were superior to the originals.*

always on hire', and the Black Boy Tavern, recalling the fashion for black page
boys. The inn fell out of favour in the 1830s because of the notorious robberies
and murders that had taken place in the nearby Black Boy Close. The
'Louden Arms' stood in Duke Street, opposite the Cattle Market. There the
Kail Club met, and a leading feature of the gathering was hare soup, for
which the house was famous.

In the early nineteenth century Glasgow's hotel centre moved to George
Square. The number of hotels in the square at various times was astonishing.
Among them were the Wellington, Star, Caledonia, Cranston's (formerly the
Royal Horse), Waverly, Crow, Clarence, Globe, Imperial, Queen's Royal and
the George, on the southeast corner of the square, which occupied part of the
site of the Municipal Buildings. When the George was taken down, it moved
to the north of the square where it remains as part of the Millennium Hotel.

The rest of the Millennium encompasses the old Queen's Hotel and the Wellington, with an extra storey added. All the other hotels have gone. When the Bank of Scotland buildings were being erected, part of the 'Crow' was taken down. Undaunted, the wag of a landlord put up a placard saying 'A wing of the Crow still open'. On either side of the entrance was a large zinc plate depicting a crow with outspread wings.

CHURCHES

To keep pace with the spiritual needs of Glasgow's growing population, many churches were built between 1707 and 1837. Before the Reformation, the city had managed with the Cathedral, Blackfriars Church and the Collegiate Church of St Mary and St Ann, erected in the Trongate about 1540. In addition, there were a number of small chapels, like St Thenew's in the region of today's St Enoch Square. When it first existed is not known, but in 1426 King James III gifted half a stone of wax for its candles. The chapel, which survived until 1597, was dedicated to the mother of St Mungo and was said to be where her bones lay. Built around 1500 was Little St Mungo's Chapel, on the north side of Gallowgate. There was also the Chapel of St Roche, or Rollox, erected around 1508 to the north of the Stable Green Port. The Chapel of the Virgin Mary on the north side of the Trongate was mentioned as early as 1293. Although it is often stated that there was a chapel dedicated to St John the Baptist at the head of Drygate, this appears to be a misconception. A property at the corner of High Street and Drygate formed one of the endowments of the Chaplainry of St John in the Cathedral and was so described in title deeds, the examination of which led to the erroneous assumption that a chapel existed there.

After the Reformation, church building began in Glasgow that led to the city having ten parish churches (including the Cathedral) by 1820. The first Protestant minister of Glasgow, David Wemyss, had no colleague until 1587 when John Cooper joined him. The two ministers shared the parish work, and on Sundays services were held in the 'Hie Kirk' and on Wednesdays and Fridays in the 'College Kirk' (old Blackfriars Church). A third minister was appointed in 1592 and given charge of the renovated Tron Church. In 1595 a fourth minister was appointed who in the following year was given charge of the landward district of Glasgow, thereafter known as the Barony Parish. (The landward district was that immediately outside the city's boundaries.) Following the division of the urban and landward congregations, in 1599 the town itself was divided into two parishes, the City and the Barony.

As the town spread west and north, St David's (Ramshorn) Church was opened in 1724 on the north side of the Cow Loan, now Ingram Street. (Replaced in 1824 by the present church.) After St David's came St Andrew's in St Andrew's Square, started in 1740 but not completed until 1756. Opposite the west end of Glasgow Green, St Andrew's Episcopal Church was built about 1756, the earliest of that denomination in Scotland. After Presbyterianism became the official religion of Scotland, prejudices ran high against Episcopalians. In Glasgow, Adam Cockburn kept a wooden chapel in a back street until 1714, when a mob tore it down and chased him out of town. Even after an Act of Toleration was passed in 1712 allowing Episcopalians to worship in their own way if they swore not to support the Stuarts, many Presbyterians ignored it.

Although five of the ten parish church buildings remain, only the Cathedral and St George's Tron in Buchanan Street are still used for church services. St George's Church originated as the Wynd Kirk, built in 1687 by some privileged Presbyterians when Episcopacy prevailed in the city. The Wynd Kirk was covered by thatch.

Apart from the ten parish churches, Glasgow had many independent churches and a Roman Catholic cathedral, St Andrews, which opened in Great Clyde Street in 1816. Of the churches built between the 1707 Union and 1837, the start of the Victorian age, very few remain.

THE OLD BARONY CHURCH, TOWNHEAD

*

The old Barony Church that was adjacent to the Cathedral is often attributed to James Adam but was more likely the work of his nephew, John Robertson. Although thought by some to be a 'lightsome and more comfortable place of worship than the Cathedral', there was no competition architecturally. The old Barony was an ugly mixture of Gothic and Baronial and had almost the appearance of a cement building, the walls being roughcast. No one had a good word to say about it until it was about to be demolished. The church was begun in 1789 but was not occupied until 1801 when the Barony congregation moved from its dismal accommodation in the Cathedral's Crypt where it had worshipped since 1595. The Barony Parish was the most populous in Scotland, reaching from the Kelvin Water in the north to the Clyde almost at Rutherglen. In the east, a line to the west of Airdrie bounded it, and in the west it stretched almost to Inch Castle on the lower Clyde.

The Old Barony Church.

An early Barony minister was Zachary Boyd, best known for preaching such an abusive sermon against Oliver Cromwell in 1650 as the latter sat in the congregation that Captain Thurlow, the general's secretary, wanted to shoot Boyd where he stood. Boyd's successor, Donald Cargill, was hanged for his association with the Covenanters. Dr John Burns was the Barony minister for seventy-two years and the last to preach in the Crypt. Dr Norman McLeod was much admired, and under his ministry the church became famous as a centre for Highlanders who had migrated to Glasgow.

The old Barony was demolished in 1889 and replaced with today's Barony Church in Castle Street (now the ceremonial hall of Strathclyde University), built by Sir J. J. Burnet and John A. Campbell in 1886.

West George Street
Independent Church
*

The site chosen in 1818 for this church was a disused filled-in quarry, and in order to get a foundation on the solid rock it was necessary to dig out all the

West George Street Independent Church.

loose material. Among the debris were the remains of a Presbyterian church that had been pulled down and thrown into the quarry. One day the minister of this church asked his great friend, Dr Ralph Wardlaw, how his proposed new church was getting on. Wardlaw explained that the difficulty was in finding a foundation. 'Ay, Dr Wardlaw, I doubt it's not easy to get a foundation for Independency in Scotland,' was the jocular rejoinder. 'Not till we get quit of all your Presbyterian rubbish,' Wardlaw readily responded.

At a cost of £10,000, Wardlaw's Independent Church opened in 1819 with room for 1,600 worshippers. Designed by James Gillespie Graham, the frontage had a pedimented Roman-Doric portico and corners faced with a pair of fluted pilasters. Not everyone appreciated the impressive frontage, however. Some resolute independents gravely objected to it, calling it almost sinfully fanciful. Others denounced it as a 'Popish Chapel'. Apparently, Queen Victoria admired the building when she passed it during her visit to the city in 1849. The interior was as elegant as the frontage, particularly the ceiling, formed into a magnificent groined arch with an elliptical opening in

The former St James' Parish Church shortly before it was demolished and
when it was reduced to being used as a warehouse.

the centre that acted as a ventilator.

In 1842 the Edinburgh and Glasgow Railway Company opened its terminus immediately adjoining the church and in 1848 bought it for £12,000 to convert into offices. The money enabled the congregation to build, at the corner of Bath Street and Pitt Street, a much more magnificent structure known as Elgin Place Chapel, which still stands although it is not used as a place of worship. The West George Street Church was demolished in 1975 to make way for an office block.

St James' Church of Scotland, London Road

*

St James' Church was the last of the city's ten parish churches. It was built in 1816 for the Methodists but was far beyond their means. When the Methodists vacated the building, the Council bought it, and in 1820 it became the parish church for the newly created parish of St James. St James' did not look like a church. It was an undignified, plain building with no classical portico or spire like most other city churches had. Stone-built, it was rectangular in plan, two storeys high and to the front had six windows on each storey, the lower ones arched. In between the windows were giant Ionic pilasters supporting an entablature in the centre of which was a pediment decorated at the apex and angles. The entablature had a balustrade over the outer windows. There were further windows above the arched entrances flanking either side of the church. The building, which sat directly opposite the Gothic Church of St Alphonsus, was damaged by fire and demolished in January 1988.

GREYFRIARS UNITED SECESSION
CHURCH, ALBION STREET
*

The ins and outs of Scottish nonconformity are extremely difficult to unravel, but the first secession from the Church of Scotland was in 1733, the result of a sermon preached at Perth on 10 October 1732 before the Synod of Perth and Stirling by the Moderator, the Reverend Ebenezer Erskine. Erskine bewailed the backslidings of the Church from the covenanted faith and practice and denounced the party in power as rejecters of Christ. Erskine and three ministers who had taken his part lost their charges and founded the Secession Church. They were Seceders, not Dissenters.

In 1783 an association of Praying Societies in and about Glasgow requested to be acknowledged by the Associated Synod (the original Secession Church). At first they met in Camphill, near Cathcart, but subsequently a chapel was built in Inkle Factory Lane off High Street. While this was being built, they met in a tent erected on the north side of Rottenrow. In 1742 a more commodious place of worship was built in Shuttle Street. In 1747 the Seceders quarrelled amongst themselves about the form of Burgess Oath in use in Edinburgh, Glasgow and Perth, and split into two branches, the Burghers and Anti-Burghers. The Shuttle Street Church became known as the Burgher Church.

In 1821 the congregation built a new church in North Albion Street on what was once part of the site of a thirteenth-century Franciscan Greyfriars Monastery. The excavation of the ground revealed what were thought to be

Right.
Greyfriars United Secession Church, Albion Street

the bones of the old Grey Friars, who had had a graveyard adjoining their monastery. Architect John Baird I, only twenty-two years old, designed the new Greyfriars Church, as it was aptly named. The portico was one of the finest in the city. It had four fluted Roman-Doric columns with corresponding pilasters supporting a massive entablature and pediment. So successful was Baird's idea of grafting a classical portico on to a plain meeting house that it continued in varying forms for the next seventy-five years. Inside the plan was traditional, with 1,500 people seated in the area and in a gallery around three sides. The dignified and important-looking Greyfriars was a departure from the usual plain, functional appearance of Secession meeting houses. Like many city churches, Greyfriars suffered from a falling membership and after being closed for some time, it was demolished in the late 1960s. The ancient site of the Grey Friars is now a car park.

ST ENOCH CHURCH,
ST ENOCH SQUARE
*

When the city expanded westwards from Stockwell, the need was felt for a west-end church. The site chosen was the ground on which there were remnants of the ancient Chapel of St Thenew. James Jaffrey's design for the church in 1780 was oblong with a spire. While this was being built, a gust of wind caused the scaffolding to sway, and in panic a worker jumped off and was killed. The entrance door, facing up Buchanan Street, had a portico of four coupled Doric pillars. On each side of the portico was a window and another above each on the upper storey. Inside were galleries on three sides and room for 822 people.

With the rapid growth of the city westwards, the new church soon became too small and it was decided to demolish it and build another on the site that could seat 1,300 people, an extra 478. In 1827, a new building designed by David Hamilton replaced the old church. It was Italian Renaissance in style and a projecting Ionic portico on the north front replaced Jaffrey's Doric one. While Hamilton's building was elegant, as it incorporated the spire of the old church, it did not look quite right. It provided an important focal point in and around the square, however, and successfully ended the vista looking down Buchanan Street.

Until the 1880s a railing enclosed the church. Once, a similar railing

Right.
Etching of St Enoch's Church, St Enoch Square, by D. Y. Cameron.

ST ENOCH'S
CHURCH

enclosed the plot of ground in the centre of the square. When, however, the buildings around the square became wholly occupied by businesses, the increased traffic caused, first, the removal of the railing round the centre plot and then that around the church. Fifty years previously the centre of the square had been enclosed and planted with leafy shrubs, wealthy people had lived in the elegant houses and a fashionable congregation had filled the church.

To considerable protest, St Enoch's Church was demolished in 1925, leaving the pretty but diminutive Travel Centre by James Miller to close the vista down Buchanan Street.

St Paul's Parish Church, John Street

*

The origins of St Paul's Church lie in the Cathedral when, after the Reformation, it was divided into three churches, the Barony, the Inner High and the Outer High. The Barony occupied the crypt, the Inner High (the High Church) the choir and the Outer High the nave. In the 1830s it was decided to restore the Cathedral and as a start a new building was put up to house the Outer High congregation in John Street. The Barony had moved out of the Crypt in 1801.

As David Hamilton did not have to incorporate parts of an existing building, as he had had to do in his St Enoch Church, he was able to produce one of his most successful churches. The frontage, which stood forward from the main building, had four Ionic pillars supporting a portico without a pediment. Above was an unusual tower, the last part of which was Doric with pediment and pilasters, with a dome capping the circular part above. The church was opened in 1836, the congregation having worshipped in the Cathedral from 1648. In 1906 the church was demolished, as the site was required for an extension of the Royal Technical College, now the University of Strathclyde.

Other churches built between 1707 and 1837 and demolished were: Anderston Relief, Greyfriars Wynd Peculiar Independent, Dovehill, Ingram Street Gaelic, George Street Baptist, South Woodside, Calton, Duke Street Gaelic and Anderston Chapel.

Left.
St Paul's Parish Church, John Street.

APPROCHING
THE VICTORIAN AGE

Glasgow approaching the Victorian age was no longer the small, homely, provincial old town with a population of 12,000 it had been at the time of the Union. It had changed into a city of nearly a quarter of a million people, its streets containing handsome mansions covering vast spaces that a few years before had been cornfields and orchards. Fashionable residences became warehouses or housing for the thousands of people who flooded into the city to work in the cotton industry and the heavy industries of chemicals and iron production. By 1820 Glasgow had 50 steam-powered mills; by 1825, 18 iron foundries; and by 1830, 27 furnaces producing about 37,500 tons of pig iron annually. Of the 310 steam engines that were at work in the Glasgow area by 1825, 176 were in the textile industry, 68 in steamships, 58 in collieries, 7 in quarries and 1 in an ironworks. By 1840 Charles Tennent's chemical works at St Rollox was the largest in Europe. An important industry had begun in 1780 when John and Robert Tennent founded a public brewery at Wellpark. Previously, citizens had brewed their ale, or 'yill' as it was called, privately.

The population explosion between 1801 (77,385) and 1831 (202,426 including suburbs) was attributed to immigration from the Highlands, rural areas and Ireland. (The Irish could come over by a cheap sixpenny deck passage on the steamboats.) By 1831 it was estimated that there were around 163,000 Scots, 3,000 English, 36,000 Irish and about 500 foreigners in Glasgow. The Glasgow Jewish community was formed in 1823, and by 1831 there were 47 Jews in the city.

Despite the rapid growth of industry, Glasgow at the beginning of the nineteenth century was still a pleasant place to live, as it was not until the 1820s and 30s that the smoke spewing from the hundreds of factory chimneys began to pollute the air and blacken the buildings.

Glasgow had become Scotland's main population centre by 1821, with 147,043 people against Edinburgh's 138,235. As it had also passed the population figures of all other towns in the British Empire, except London, it was entitled to call itself the Second City of the Empire, which is how it entered the Victorian age.

CHAPTER 4
THE VICTORIAN CITY
1837–1901

✳

The year Queen Victoria came to the throne, 1837, was troublesome for Glasgow. During the early months the weather was bitterly cold and for several weeks the Clyde was frozen over. A typhus epidemic killed over 4,000 people, and for fourteen weeks during the spring and summer the cotton-spinners were on strike over proposed savage pay cuts. When employers brought in blackleg labour, the strikers rioted, setting mills on fire and attacking loyal workers. One of these workers, Irishman Adam Smith, an employee at Houldsworth's mill in Anderston, was shot dead on 22 July. In the following January, five office bearers of the Association of Operative Cotton-Spinners of Glasgow and Neighbourhood, who had orchestrated the strike, were brought before the High Court on charges ranging from being members of a secret association to illegally raise wages and control disputes to murder. Although the murder charge was 'not proven', the defendants were found guilty of other offences and were sentenced to seven years' transportation. The sentence was never carried out and after a public campaign they were pardoned in 1841.

STREETSCAPE AND BUILDINGS

The Glasgow of the 1840s was roughly the size of the city now contained within the inner ring road (the M8 north of the river). There was much building going on, such as the four-storey tenements for which the city became famous. The Georgian city centre had been much altered. A report in the *Glasgow Herald* of 1843 said: 'Since the meetings of the British Association of 1840, the new public buildings erected had included the stations for the Edinburgh-Glasgow, Glasgow-Ayr, the Glasgow-Greenock Railways, the Western Club, the Linen Bank, the Western Bank, the Union Bank, The Glasgow and Ship Bank, the Merchants House, the City Hall, the Corn

Exchange, the Gartnavel Lunatic Asylum, twelve Presbyterian Churches and one Catholic Chapel.' Not mentioned was the large, grandiose neoclassical City and County Buildings erected in Wilson Street in 1842. Among important buildings erected before 1840 were Hutchesons' Hospital in Ingram Street and the Royal Bank of Scotland in Royal Exchange Place, started in 1827. The Necropolis had been laid out in 1833 and was ongoing. Victorian Glasgow pioneered iron-framed buildings, the most famous being the former Gardner's warehouse in Jamaica Street, designed by John Baird in 1855.

Unlike the rows about the demolition of the Cathedral Towers, there were no complaints when the simple eighteenth-century buildings were replaced with magnificent public and commercial buildings proclaiming the wealth of the city. The Council and speculators of the mid-1850s were laying the foundations of a town that today is regarded as the foremost Victorian city in the world.

While public and commercial building could not be faulted, housebuilding could be, as it had not managed to keep pace with the flood of newcomers, most of whom lodged in airless, overcrowded unsanitary hovels in the vennels and wynds of the old part of the city where rents were cheapest. (With the serious recessions of trade in 1816, 1819 and 1826, many incomers, and citizens, could not find work and could afford only the most wretched accommodation.) The wynds were at first the streets, clean though narrow, between the well-built mansions with their gardens and orchards. Later, the green places were built over and the wynds became arteries to long winding 'closes' into which were densely packed the degenerates of the city. As an example, as early as 1818 twenty-three of the lowest class of Irish were said to be living in two rooms with only three beds. Sometimes 300 shared one common stair with no form of sanitation. The five- and six-roomed houses that had once belonged to the wealthy had been divided into as many dwellings as possible, one room being allocated to one family. Housing was almost totally in the hands of private landlords, and by the 1840s there were more than 600 common lodging houses with about 10,000 inhabitants.

Glasgow fared badly in reports on housing in Great Britain. In 1839, the author of a Parliamentary Report on Housing in Great Britain wrote: 'I have seen human degradation in some of the worst places, both in England and abroad, but I did not believe until I had visited the wynds of Glasgow that so large an amount of filth, crime, misery and disease existed in one spot in any civilised country.'

Not only outsiders were appalled by the extent of the decline in the old city. The city's Chief Constable, addressing the British Association in 1840, said:

In the interior part of the square bounded on the west by
Stockwell Street, on the north by Trongate, on the south by the
river and in the east by the High Street, there is concentrated
everything that is wretched, dissolute, loathsome and pestilential.
These places are filled by many thousands of miserable creatures.
The houses are unfit even for styes, and every apartment is filled
with a promiscuous crowd of men, women and children, all in the
most revolting state of filth and squalor. In many of the houses
there is scarcely any ventilation and from the extremely defective
sewerage filth of every kind constantly accumulates.

The authors of a report in 1842, *The Sanitary Conditions of the Labouring
Population*, had the following to say:

It appeared to us that both the structural arrangements and the
conditions of the population in Glasgow were the worst of any we
had seen in any part of Great Britain. In the courts of Argyle
Street, there were no privies or drains and the dung heaps
received all the filth, which the swarms of wretched inhabitants
could give. We learned that a considerable part of the rents for the
houses was paid by the produce of these dung heaps . . .

Seventy per cent of the population lived in such conditions, and although the
Council tried to remedy the situation in the late 1840s by setting aside
£30,000 to buy the worst properties in the city centre and demolish them, it
resulted in new districts emerging around the city that were just as objec-
tionable as the old.

As ever more people poured into the city, the housing problem intensi-
fied. Speculators rushed to provide accommodation by throwing up cheap
tenement housing on any space behind existing properties, the 'backlands' as
they were known. Two or more rows of tenements were crammed into the
space and so crowded did these backlands and other disreputable stinking
rabbit warrens become with overbuilding that thousands of people lived with
hardly any light or air. A single close in the notorious 'Rookery' in the
Drygate housed five hundred people.

The new buildings, entered through narrow closes that led to other
closes, quickly became slums as the occupants took in lodgers, continuing
overcrowding in a new form. In addition, as the builders had not bothered
much about sewage or sanitation, diseases like cholera and typhus spread.

Typhus had occurred in 1818–19, 1831, 1837, 1846 and 1864. Cholera (cholera morbus), mainly caused by polluted water, had been absent for 200 years when it reappeared in 1832 and was almost entirely limited to the area around the Cross that was dependent on the old public wells for its water supply. Out of 6,000 cases, 2,842 died. Even more people died in an epidemic of 1848–49 that, unlike the 1832 epidemic, also affected people in wealthier areas. In an outbreak of 1853–54, 3,900 people lost their lives over a period of thirteen months. However, in 1866 (the last cholera epidemic) only 68 people died, no doubt because of the introduction of the Loch Katrine water scheme, opened by Queen Victoria in 1857.

The building of the backlands was the main reason for the wholesale destruction of the old city in the late nineteenth century.

As the attempts by the Corporation to remove the worst of the filthy, overcrowded dilapidated buildings had failed, a City Improvement Act was obtained from parliament in 1866, creating a City Improvement Trust. The preamble of the Act stated:

> Whereas various portions of the City of Glasgow are so built, and
> the buildings thereon are so densely inhabited as to be injurious to
> the moral and physical welfare of the Inhabitants, and many of the
> thoroughfares are narrow, circuitous and inconvenient and it
> would be of public and local advantage if various houses and
> buildings were taken down, and those portions of the said City
> reconstituted, and new streets were constructed in and through
> various parts of the said City and several of the existing streets
> altered, widened, and diverted and that, in connection with the
> reconstitution of those portions of the city, provision were made
> for dwellings for the labouring classes who may be displaced in
> consequence thereof.

The congested areas, covering 90 acres and with a population of over 50,000, were in, or immediately contiguous to, that portion of the city known as 'Old Glasgow', including parts of Calton and the Gorbals. The Act empowered the Corporation to form thirty-nine new streets and to realign twelve others; to

Left.
This photograph of the corner of Duke Street and High Street in 1897 shows the backlands at their very worst. The buildings across from each other practically touch and the entrance to the dwellings was through an airless, lightless tunnel. Shortly after the photograph was taken, the buildings were demolished.

compulsorily acquire old properties and demolish them; to dispose of the ground released on lease or feu; and to control rebuilding. In addition, the Act allowed the Corporation to acquire land for the purposes of rehousing the dispossessed tenants and to erect and maintain on any of the lands acquired by it such dwelling houses for mechanics, labourers and other persons of the working and poorer classes.

As the Trust's work got underway, the acquiring of substandard buildings became more costly than was first thought, resulting in the Trust temporarily improving some of its old properties and converting a couple of mills to provide accommodation for the evicted tenants. A method employed by the Trust to house those termed 'the dregs of the population', who had lodged in the worst parts of the old town, was to build common lodging houses, or 'models' as they were known. Seven were built between 1871 and 1884, six for males and one for females. Each lodger had an enclosed sleeping cubicle with a comfortable bed.

As another attempt to prevent overcrowding, a system of 'ticketed houses' was introduced in 1866, the same year as the Improvement Trust was set up. All houses of three apartments or fewer and not exceeding 2,000 cubic feet were measured and had a metal plate (a token) fixed to the door stating the number of occupants allowed by law – a ratio of 300 cubic feet for every person over eight years of age. By the 1880s, there were 23,228 ticketed houses of which 16,413 were single apartments. When, without warning, night sanitary inspectors visited ticketed houses, people were discovered in cupboards and under beds. One inspector found eleven adults in a house and seven more hiding on the roof. The property of 880 cubic feet was designated for only three people. Often two tiers of people were in the same bed, one under the mattress and one on top.

When a demand for improved commercial premises led to the creation of a new business district around St Vincent Street, the Blythswood district became less desirable and the middle-class people who had moved there fled farther west. South Woodside, west of Sauchiehall Street, had been started in the late 1830s with streets such as Newton Place, Woodside Crescent, Place and Terrace and Lyndoch Street. Lyndoch Crescent, begun in 1845, was the last part of the development. Woodlands Hill was laid out in the 1830s and 40s and was crowned in the 1850s by Charles Wilson's magnificent Park area, said

Right.
The Drygate Model Lodging House, built in 1869 at a cost of £3,426,
the first of the seven common lodging houses built by the Improvement Trust
to house single people (men initially).

to be the finest piece of architectural planning of the mid-nineteenth century.

Glasgow's longest, straightest and finest thoroughfare, Great Western Road, was a toll road authorised by Act of Parliament in 1836. It opened in 1841, and the first of its great terraces was Charles Wilson's Kirklee, originally Windsor, begun in 1845 but not finished until 1864. Then came J. T. Rochead's Venetian-style Grosvenor Terrace in 1855, followed by Belhaven Terrace and, in 1870, Alexander 'Greek' Thomson's magnificent Great Western Terrace.

In 1842 the Botanic Gardens were moved from the west end of Sauchiehall Street to a site lying between Great Western Road and the south bank of the River Kelvin. In 1853 work began on Kelvingrove Park, first known as the West End Park. To form the park, the council paid £77,945 in 1852 for the estates of Kelvingrove and Woodlands. Later, parts of the lands of Nether Newton, Clayslaps and Gilmorehill were added, increasing the park area from 66 acres to 87 acres.

As Glasgow's industrial affluence grew, so did the West End, with the creation of districts such as Hyndland, Kelvinside, Dowanhill, Dowanside and Hillhead, a burgh from 1869 to 1891 when Glasgow annexed it. Hillhead began in the early part of the nineteenth century as a garden suburb of villas and then changed about mid-century to terraces and tenements of an exceptionally high standard.

The introduction of public transport had made it easier for people to move to outlying districts. Although the pioneer was Robert Frame, who began a horse-drawn omnibus service between Bridgeton and Anderston on 1 January 1845, the most successful operator in Glasgow was Andrew Menzies, who in 1849 launched his Menzies tartan-painted omnibuses that ran not only within the city but also to the outskirts. It was Menzies who realised that tramlines would allow buses to run quicker and smoother, and in 1869–70, the Corporation carried out the laying of rails for the Glasgow Tramway and Omnibus Co., formed by Menzies with himself as managing director. Glasgow's first tram ran in 1872 from St George's Cross to Eglinton Toll. The Corporation took over the tramway service in 1894.

The consequence of Glasgow's industrial and commercial activity was a building boom between 1860 and the end of the century. In that period there was plenty of money to be spent on luxurious building materials and ornamentation, and the buildings erected in the city centre reflected this. Public buildings, banks, insurance offices, warehouses and even factories

Left.
Woodside Crescent, c. 1839 and Kirklee Terrace, originally Windsor Terrace,
the first of the Great Western Road Terraces.

proclaimed the city's wealth. Furthermore, it was Glasgow's good fortune to have on hand a group of architects of outstanding merit whose combined talents, according to Lord Esher in 1971 in his *Conservation in Glasgow*, made the city 'the finest surviving example of a great Victorian city'. Among these architects were Charles Wilson, John Burnet, John Baird, J. T. Rochead, James Sellars, John Honeyman and Alexander 'Greek' Thomson. Building styles were diverse – Scots Baronial for the City of Glasgow Bank, Gothic for the Stock Exchange, Italianate for the Merchants House and the Commercial Bank, Venetian for the Ca'd'Oro, Grecian for the Grosvenor. The lavish City Chambers, said by its architect, William Young, to be a 'free and dignified treatment of the Italian Renaissance', exemplified more than any other building the city's wealth and importance.

To make them more impressive, some earlier buildings, like the Merchants House and the Trustees Savings Bank, had storeys added. Others were given a new frontage, like the Union Bank. Later in the century, however, many mid-century offices were replaced by office blocks that were taller but not wider as they were usually rebuilt on the existing plot. After 1880, building regulations, along with the introduction of lifts, permitted heights up to 100 feet. By this time, the earlier favoured Classical and Italian Renaissance styles were being replaced with what was called the modern French style found in the Sun Fire and Life Insurance building in West George Street and the Glasgow Evening Citizen building in St Vincent Place, among the first in the city to be built of red sandstone.

Just making it into the Victorian age were Glasgow Art Nouveau buildings, many having narrow frontages as they were redeveloped on Georgian house plots. A splendid example of Glasgow Art Nouveau is the building in St Vincent Street known as the 'Hatrack' because of the shape of the projecting finials on its rooftop cupola. Built within a single house plot, the nine-storey and attic building has a facade mainly of glass held within a stone skeleton heavy with Art Nouveau elements. Designed in 1899 by James Salmon II and J. Gaff Gillespie, the foremost architects of Glasgow Art Nouveau, the ornamentation is unlike anything else in the city.

By the end of the nineteenth century, Glasgow's most innovative architect, Charles Rennie Mackintosh, was beginning to make his mark, and in 1899 the first part of his masterpiece, The Glasgow School of Art, was finished.

All the above buildings remain but, sadly, the following, which were just as outstanding, do not.

BANKS

Glasgow did not have any banks until the middle of the eighteenth century. The Bank of Scotland had tried to open branches in the city in 1696 and 1731 but both failed and it was not until 1749 that Glasgow's first bank, The Glasgow and Ship, opened in the Bridgegate. Hot on its heels was the Glasgow Arms, also in the Bridgegate, which opened in 1750. It failed in 1793. Next came the Thistle in Virginia Street in 1761 and after that the Merchant Banking Company in 1769. The above were all private banks. In 1783 the Royal Bank of Scotland established a branch in Glasgow, with David Dale acting as its agent from his shop in Hopkirk's Land in High Street. From then on, various banks were established, such as the British Linen, the Commercial, the National, the Western, the National Security Savings, the Savings Bank, the Clydesdale and the City of Glasgow, whose failure caused a scandal. At first, the various banks operated from modest premises, but as their business grew, they progressed to more imposing ones, culminating in the Victorian era when they erected magnificent banking halls to show their wealth and importance. As well as giving an impression of wealth and grandeur, the buildings had also to convey solidity, a most important quality for a bank to present to the public. Although many of these splendid Victorian banks remain, albeit with renovated interiors, modern buildings have replaced others.

British Linen Bank,
Queen Street
*

The British Linen Bank opened in Glasgow in May 1818 in an old mansion house at 71 Queen Street. The bank stayed there until 1842 when it moved into a new building occupying a prestigious site at the corner of Queen Street and Ingram Street overlooking the Royal Exchange. As, then, David Hamilton was the city's favourite bank architect, having already designed banks for the Union, Western and the Clydesdale, the British Linen commissioned him to design their new principal Glasgow office. Hamilton gave the bank an Italian Renaissance-style building, three storeys and basement in height, with a beautifully rounded corner portion flanked by double pilasters and massive consoles. All the windows had richly ornamented headings and those at the first-floor level had small balconies. The cornice was topped with a balustrade.

The British Linen Bank.

To increase office space, the proportions of the building were spoiled in 1903 when two storeys that did not match the original architecture were added above the balustrade. Also added was a corner dome flanked by two statues. Hamilton had intended to have a corner dome and statues placed along the balustrade but, at £30,000, the building had cost enough without adding to it. The delightful old bank was demolished in 1968 and a modern building put up in its place.

UNION BANK, INGRAM STREET
*

The Glasgow Union Bank, as it was first known, originated in 1830. It was the first bank in the city to be formed on the joint-stock principle. It became the Union Bank of Scotland in 1843 by which time it had acquired the Thistle Bank, Paisley Union, William Forbes & Co. of Edinburgh, Hunter & Co. of Ayr and the Glasgow and Ship Bank Co. These amalgamations made the Union a national bank of major status. After an amalgamation of no fewer than thirteen partnership banks, the Union merged with the Bank of Scotland in 1955.

Union Bank, Ingram Street.

The Union's first office was in the Old Post Office Court off Trongate. Its second was in Ingram Street/Virginia Street, built on the site of the Virginia Mansion that had stood at the top of Virginia Street with its back to Ingram Street. (After the amalgamation of the Glasgow Bank Co. with the Ship Bank in 1836, the newly formed Glasgow Ship Bank demolished the mansion that had been bought by the Glasgow Bank Co. eight years previously. The new building erected on the site by David Hamilton in 1841 became the head office of the Glasgow and Ship Bank until the Union took it over as its Glasgow head office after the amalgamation of the Union with the Glasgow and Ship in 1843.)

The bank's frontage to Ingram Street consisted of a six-pillared, Roman-Doric portico raised on a high basement and supporting an ornamented entablature. Over all were six full-length statues, executed by John Mossman, representing Britannia, Wealth, Justice, Peace, Industry and Glasgow. The frontage to Virginia Street had a great painted window in three panels on which were full-length figures of James Watt, William Paterson, founder of the Bank of England, and Adam Smith. In 1876 the bank was extended and given a magnificent new facade by architect John Burnet. Mossman added two pairs of statues to those that had surmounted the old Virginia Street

The City of Glasgow Bank, Glassford Street.

portico. Hamilton's portico was removed to the Royal Princess Theatre in the Gorbals, which became the Citizens' Theatre. The Palace Theatre next door to the Royal Princess shared the portico which was destroyed in 1977. The main part of the original bank building with the domed single-storey telling hall added in 1853 by James Salmon remains.

THE CITY OF GLASGOW BANK
GLASSFORD STREET

✳

The City of Glasgow Bank was founded in 1839, and by the mid-1850s was a favourite of both the moneyed and working classes. It catered especially for small investors, branches opening in the evenings to receive deposits. At the time of the Western Bank's failure in 1857, the City of Glasgow Bank stopped payment for a few days during the panic. When calm was restored, however, it resumed business and flourished, and shareholders were delighted when the directors at the annual meeting in June 1878 reported that the bank had 133 branches, deposits of £8,000,000 and that a dividend of 12 per cent would be paid. Although some weeks later, stories spread that the bank was in trouble, nothing prepared the city for the intimation in the morning newspapers of 2 October that it had closed its doors. Some other banks agreed to honour their notes, but four days later the City went into liquidation. Upon examination, it was found that the bank's losses amounted to £6,000,000 and that the directors had concealed this by false accounting. Later it came out that the directors had also advanced unsecured loans to insolvent companies with whom they all had business connections.

The bank's failure, described as 'the greatest disaster that had ever befallen the commercial community of Great Britain', had catastrophic results commercially. Scarcely a day passed without another Glasgow firm becoming bankrupt. Those who suffered worst, however, were the shareholders as their liability was unlimited. Many with only a few hundred pounds invested were liable for thousands. (Out of 1,819 shareholders, only 250 remained solvent.) Several shareholders committed suicide. So great was the sympathy for the shareholders that the community raised nearly £400,000 as a relief fund.

The arrest, trial and conviction of the directors for criminal fraud were no consolation for those who had suffered from the gigantic fraud, the repercussions of which were far-reaching and long-lasting. One good thing came out of the disaster, however – the passing of the Companies Act of 1879 allowing banks to adopt limited liability for their shareholders.

In many suburbs there are tenement buildings that look unfinished. This was as far as they had been built when the bank failed and there was no money to finish them. The bank building itself was such a case. At the end of 1877, it had begun a large extension to its head office on the west side of Glassford Street, but the crash came before it was completed. At a cost of £20,000, it was another example of the bank overextending itself. The dignified but lavish design by James Sellars was French Renaissance. A massive six-pillared Corinthian Order linked the first and second floors, the windows being deeply recessed behind, giving an appearance of solidity and grandeur. The top floor was never finished. Instead of having the planned elaborate attic storey with corner towers, it ended with a balustraded cornice with plinths for six statues that were never erected. When the building was sold on behalf of the bank's creditors, it became the property of warehousemen Mann Byres & Co., which used a bank strong room to store its books and valuables. The building was demolished in 1959 to make way for an ordinary commercial block.

THEATRES

Although Glasgow was slow to take to theatregoing, by the 1840s it had attracted quite a following. Interestingly, the audiences came from those above and below the middle classes, who had little time for theatricals except for pantomimes. Melodramas were particularly popular among the lower classes and young men about town frequented the music halls.

During the Victorian age many theatres were built, and by the end of the nineteenth century the city had the following: the Grand (Cowcaddens), the Royal (Hope Street), the Gaiety (corner of West Nile Street and Sauchiehall Street), the Royalty (Sauchiehall Street), the Royal Princess (Gorbals), the Metropole (Stockwell Street), the Queen's (Watson Street), the Empire (Sauchiehall Street) and the Britannia (Argyle Street). There were also the Tivoli Music Halls, Hengler's and Zoo Circuses and three waxworks. Of the above, only the Royal and parts of the Britannia survive. Outside the city's boundaries was the Lyceum in Govan Road, Govan then being a burgh. Some of the above theatres started life with different names, the Metropole as the Scotia Music Hall, the Queen's as the Star Music Hall and the Grand as the Prince of Wales. Many great names of the nineteenth-century theatrical world trod the boards of Glasgow's theatres. A peculiarity of the city's theatres was that they had a tendency to burn down, and, apart from the Empire, those that follow all did.

THE THEATRE ROYAL,
DUNLOP STREET

*

John Jackson opened the first Theatre Royal in 1782 but despite bringing many great players of the time to perform there, like the legendary Mrs Siddons, by 1791 he was bankrupt. After a time as a warehouse, in 1825 the building became a theatre again, renamed the Caledonian. In the basement was another theatre, the Dominion of Fancy, run by showman John Henry Alexander.

After the Theatre Royal in Queen Street burned down in 1829, the Dunlop Street theatre was rebuilt to take the place of both and renamed the Theatre Royal. In 1839–40, architect William Spence radically rebuilt the theatre into a splendid neoclassical building of eight bays with columns, pilasters, arches and niches containing statues of Shakespeare, Garrick and John Henry Alexander, who had become the proprietor of the whole building and who had no small opinion of himself. As well as his management role,

Theatre Royal, Dunlop Street.

Alexander was an actor and played many parts.

The theatre witnessed a terrible tragedy on the evening of 17 February 1849. During the second act of *The Surrender of Calais*, somebody in the gallery irresponsibly raised a false cry of fire. Everyone rushed for the doors and 65 people, mainly youths, were trampled to death. Although there was no fire on that occasion, there was on 31 January 1863 when the whole building went up in flames. With the remarkable optimism of the Victorian age, however, the Theatre Royal was again rebuilt behind the old frontage. It re-opened on 17 December 1863 under the management of Mr and Mrs Edmund Glover but lasted for only another five years when it was sold to the City Union Railway Company for £27,500. The Dunlop Street theatre, regarded with perhaps greater affection than any other theatre in the city, closed on 18 May 1869 and soon after was demolished to allow the building of St Enoch Station to begin.

THE CITY AND ADELPHI THEATRES
*

The City and the Adelphi theatres were built on Glasgow Green near the Court House at the foot of Saltmarket.

The City Theatre
*

The flamboyant actor and conjurer John Henry Anderson, 'the Wizard of the North', opened the City Theatre, built on a narrow site between the Adelphi and Cooke's Circus, in July 1845. According to *The Scotsman*, the first night saw the largest audience ever assembled to witness a theatrical representation in Glasgow. The pit, which could hold 3,000, was crammed, as were the balconies. The total capacity of the theatre was 5,000. Although the City Theatre looked imposing, with its entrance portico of four Doric pillars, it was shoddily constructed and in November, a few months after it opened, it burned down in one of Glasgow's most spectacular fires, hot ashes being swept by the wind as far as George Square. There was no way the firemen could save the City, but they worked furiously to prevent the Adelphi Theatre alongside from suffering a similar fate. Thousands of spectators watched the proceedings.

As Anderson was only partly insured, it was said he would have rushed into the flames in the hope of saving some of his property if he had not been restrained. He was suspicious about how the fire had started as 60,000 citizens had signed a petition against him building his theatre in Glasgow Green.

The Adelphi Theatre
*

The Adelphi, saved from the City Theatre fire in 1845, had opened in December 1842. It was the first theatre to be erected in Scotland after the passing of the new Licensing Act. While it looked substantial and was very spacious, accommodating nearly 2,000 people, it was mainly constructed of timber and when it went on fire in November 1848, the fire spread so rapidly that before the fire engines arrived the whole building was ablaze and obviously could not be saved. Apparently, when the flames broke out, the company was rehearsing a new piece, *The Ocean Monarch*, or *The Ship of Fire*. It was said that the theatre was badly constructed at the outset and had undergone so many alterations and reconstructions that over £10,000 had been spent on it from first to last. What caused the fire remained a mystery,

Opposite top.
The ruins of the City Theatre, from a watercolour by William Simpson.

Opposite bottom.
The Adelphi Theatre on fire, watched by thousands of spectators.
To the left is the Court House at the foot of Saltmarket.

as no fire was known to be in the theatre at the time of the accident. The building was not insured.

The remaining building on the site, Cooke's Circus, elegant and substantial, but entirely built of timber, burned down a couple of weeks after the Adelphi.

QUEEN'S THEATRE, WATSON STREET

*

While the Queen's Theatre in Watson Street near Glasgow Cross burned down, unlike the Adelphi and the City it had had a long and varied life. It began in 1878 as the Star Music Hall, became the Shakespeare Music Hall, the New Star Theatre of Varieties, the People's Palace of Amusements, Pringle's Picture Palace and, finally, the Queen's Variety Theatre.

Like some other Glasgow theatres, the Queen's did not occupy the whole of a building – it was formed out of the upper floors of an unprepossessing four-storey warehouse block. Although unprepossessing on the outside, the interior was ornate, with two balconies encrusted with fruity plaster garlands.

On 1 November 1884 disaster struck the New Star Theatre of Varieties, as the theatre had become the previous month. Just as had happened in the Dunlop Street Theatre thirty-five years earlier, there was a false alarm of fire, and in the panic to get out of the theatre, fourteen people were trampled to death on the stairs. The theatre remained closed until November 1892, when, renamed the People's Palace of Varieties, it was advertised as 'The Most Popular Hall in the City'. In 1902 Glasgow Corporation bought the warehouse and therefore the theatre, which had had another name change to the Queen's Theatre of Varieties. Capacity was reduced from 2,620 to 1,800. In 1907 the theatre was leased to cinema pioneer Ralph Pringle and temporarily renamed Pringle's Picture Palace. The seating layout was not suitable for a cinema, however, and by the end of the First World War the Queen's had reverted to operating as a music hall whose productions had an earthy, bawdy flavour.

During the 1930s the combination of ribald scripts in broad Glaswegian dialect and the talents of Frank and Doris Droy and Sammy Murray packed the audiences in. It was said that the only reason the vulgar scripts were passed by the Lord Chamberlain (who until the 1960s censored theatrical scripts) was that no one but a Glaswegian could understand them. The

The Queen's Theatre, photographed the morning after the fire.

Queen's reputation for hilarious, earthy performances continued until a fire in 1952 irreparably destroyed the dressing rooms, stage and ceiling. Shortly afterwards the building was demolished.

ROYALTY THEATRE, SAUCHIEHALL STREET

*

During 1879–80 a palatial French Renaissance-style block designed by James Thomson containing shops, offices and a hotel was erected on the corner of Sauchiehall Street and Renfield Street. Behind was the Royalty Theatre, entered through ornate arches at the corner of the block. Thomson did not

The Royalty Theatre, Sauchiehall Street.

design the delightful French Renaissance-style theatre. It was the work of Frank Matcham, a well-known London theatre designer. Although the Royalty's capacity was given as nearly 2,000, patrons must have been very cramped as the theatre was small, the circle having only seven rows.

The Royalty opened on 24 December 1879 under the ownership and management of Mr E. L. Knapp. In 1884 Knapp sold the theatre, generally considered the premier theatre in Glasgow, to Howard and Wyndham, who in turn sold it to the Scottish Playhouse Company for use as a repertory theatre. It was renamed the Lyric. During the First World War the entire block, including the theatre, was sold to the YMCA, which used the theatre as a cinema to entertain the troops. After the war, the theatre reverted to amateur dramatics. In 1935 the YMCA formed the Lyric Players, who until 1940 presented two seasons a year in the theatre. In 1946 the Players resumed their performances.

In 1953 the Lyric went up in flames. The owners, however, decided to rebuild it, and at a cost of £112,000 a new, less opulent Lyric, with seating reduced to 847, rose from the ashes. The rebuild, however, had a shortfall of £25,600, and as the decade progressed the YMCA's finances became so stretched that in 1959 it sold the whole block and the theatre to developers for £300,000. In 1962 the lot was demolished to make way for St Andrew's House, an ugly concrete office block in vogue at that time.

THE EMPIRE THEATRE, SAUCHIEHALL STREET
*

Almost directly across the road from the Royalty was the Empire Theatre, a rarity among Glasgow's theatres as it did not go on fire. It was also the best known of Glasgow's music halls outside the city. The Empire was built on the site of the old Gaiety Theatre, which stood on the corner of West Nile Street and Sauchiehall Street. Although the Gaiety opened in 1874 as a legitimate theatre, after a change of ownership it became a music hall that was so successful that it was decided to build a much larger theatre. Like the Royalty, the new Empire Palace, as it was called, was the work of Frank Matcham, who designed it in his usual opulent French Renaissance style at a cost of £30,000. The Empire Palace opened on 5 April 1897 with imperson-ator Vesta Tilley heading the bill. Although it is not known exactly when the theatre became known as the Empire, in 1901 a new 'Empire' name sign was erected. Most of the famous names of British music hall appeared at the Empire, and so popular did it become that it closed in August 1930 for a major reconstruction to make room for more seating. Unfortunately, during the reconstruction, the fabulous Matcham interior was removed, as were the dome, turrets and minarets on the facade, to accommodate an extra storey. The result was a mammoth hotchpotch of a building with 2,100 seats.

When the new Empire opened on 28 September 1931 with Jack Payne's Band, then the most popular in Britain, topping the bill, the decor was described as 'restrained classic ornament, the colour motif is scrumbled ivory with sub-themes of plum and silver, and the draperies and upholstery are in Rose du Barry with silver satin appliqué work'.

The Glasgow Empire had a reputation as the 'English comics' grave-yard'. English comedians just did not appeal to West of Scotland audiences and many 'died' on stage. Other English performers, however, like Frankie Vaughan, Max Bygraves, Harry Secombe and pop idols like Cliff Richard, Adam Faith and Marty Wilde got a warm welcome. So did American stars like Frank Sinatra, Bob Hope, Abbot and Costello, Dean Martin and Jerry Lewis, Danny Kaye, Betty Hutton, Judy Garland and Dorothy Lamour who appeared at the Empire in the 1950s. Glaswegians loved the thrill of seeing

The Empire Theatre, Sauchiehall Street.

their screen idols in the flesh. American crooners like Johnnie Ray, Dickie Valentine and Guy Mitchell always played to packed houses. Scottish talent, like Andy Stewart in 'The Andy Stewart Show', also filled the theatre.

At the beginning of 1963 the theatre's owners, Moss Empires Ltd, decided to sell the building to developers for demolition, because, according to them, it was uneconomical to run. The last performance, on Sunday 31 March 1963, was spectacular and emotional as everyone knew that the theatre was closing not because of lack of patronage but because the owners wanted to profit from it. Britain's second largest variety theatre was demolished immediately after the final show and was replaced by an unattractive, characterless office development.

CHURCHES

In 1840 there were 85 places of worship in Glasgow, 40 belonging to the Church of Scotland, 39 to the dissenters, 4 to Episcopalians and 2 to the Roman Catholics. After the Disruption of 1843 (a church/state conflict), however, when about a third of the Church of Scotland left to form the Free Church, and the formation in 1847 of the United Presbyterians by those who had already seceded from the Church of Scotland, there was a rush by the rival denominations to build places of worship. Churches were appearing all over the city, and if one denomination built one on such and such a street, a rival would put up a much grander one across the road.

In 1850 a statistical survey of church denominations revealed the following: Church of Scotland 29, Free Church 32, United Presbyterians 27, other Secession churches 14, Roman Catholic 6, Episcopalian 6, Baptists 5, Methodists 2. By 1880 there were 331 churches in Glasgow and its suburbs and 31 denominations, the largest groups being: Church of Scotland 78; Free Church 78; United Presbyterian 64; Roman Catholic 18. There were also 8 Plymouth Brethren churches. In 1900 the United Presbyterians and the Free Churches united to form the United Free (UF) Church, which rejoined the Church of Scotland in 1929.

As there have been about 200 Victorian churches demolished in Glasgow to date, to detail them all is obviously impossible. The four featured represent a cross-section of architectural styles and denominations. Two were in the city centre, one in the east end and one in the west end. All were a loss to the city. To be fair, however, with churches uniting, a population shift away from the city centre and a fall in church attendances in the twentieth century, many places of worship were left empty and, as they were becoming derelict and the owners did not have the funds to maintain them, for safety there was no option other than to demolish them. Nevertheless, as city centre sites commanded high prices for development, often the buildings were demolished purely for profit, robbing Glasgow's skyline of their steeples, such a striking feature of the inner city. Although it is not always possible, some churches have been successfully converted to secular use, like the Ramshorn, now a theatre, Cowcaddens Parish Church, now The Piping Centre, and Elgin Place Church, now a nightclub.

Renfield St Stephen's in Bath Street, still used in a religious capacity, was created by a union of thirteen churches – Blythswood, Buccleuch, Cowcaddens, Grant Street, Lyon Street, Milton, Port Dundas, Renfield Street, St George's Road, St Matthew's, St Stephen's, St Stephen's West and Shamrock Street.

RENFIELD STREET UNITED
PRESBYTERIAN CHURCH
*

The above church was built on the corner of Renfield Street and Sauchiehall Street. It opened in August 1848 and was unlike any other church in the city. It had no spire but, instead, many pinnacles reached skywards. James Brown was the architect of the perpendicular Gothic-style building that, with its profusion of arcading, many large windows and distinctive pinnacles, was considered too exaggerated for a church belonging to a dissenting body. Considering the building's lavishness, its high cost of £13,000 is understandable. The exceptionally graceful iron and timber interior matched the style and magnificence of the exterior. Supported by delicate cast-iron pillars, the ceiling had ribbed plaster vaulting over both nave and gallery aisles. Tall windows lit a three-sided chancel containing a pulpit raised high above floor level. Like so many other city churches, Renfield became too expensive to maintain and the congregation reluctantly sold it to developers who demolished it in 1963. The loss of the delightful interior was particularly regrettable.

RENFIELD FREE CHURCH,
BATH STREET
*

From one Renfield Church to another. This one belonged to the Free Church and the reason for it being called Renfield when it was in Bath Street was that Renfield Street was its first site and when a new church was built at the corner of Elmbank Street and Bath Street the original name was transferred to it. Very confusing. Boucher and Cousland were the architects of the new church, started in 1857 and opened in May 1858. The structure had an elaborate Gothic facade and a tall corner tower with octagonal upper stages, the

Right.
Renfield Street United Presbyterian Church.

Overleaf left.
Renfield Free Church, Bath Street.

Overleaf right.
Park Parish Church and its steeple, which, along with the three steeples of Charles Wilson's Free Church College, dominate the skyline of the Park area and are famous city sights.

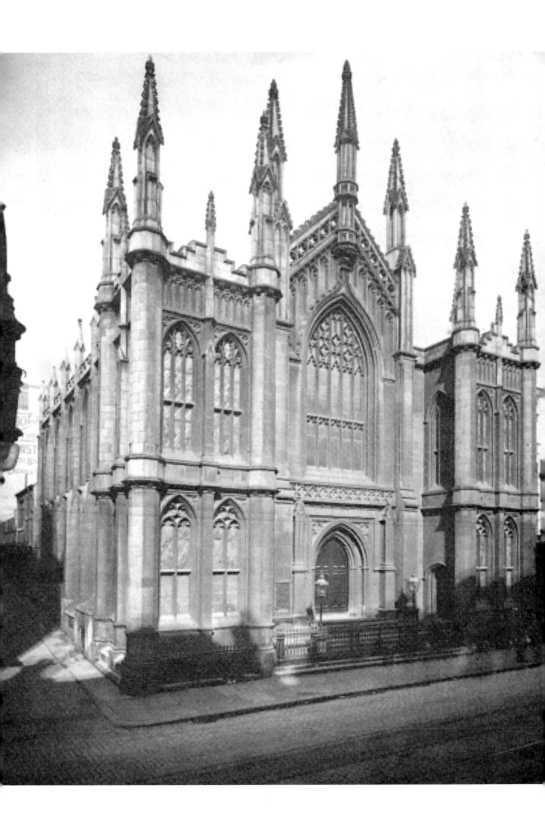

only one of its kind in the city. (The parapet suffered storm damage in 1962.) Above the main doorway was an elaborate rose window. The interior had a three-aisle plan, and the graceful cast-iron columns supporting the galleries continued upwards to support a superb open-timber roof. (The cast-iron columns were most likely the work of the Saracen Foundry of Possilpark as Boucher was closely associated with it and introduced decorative ironwork on many of his buildings, such as 22 Park Circus whose interior he designed for the owner of the foundry, Walter MacFarlane.)

After the United Free Church rejoined the Church of Scotland in 1929, the new organisation found it had surplus buildings, and in the 1930s it sold the Bath Street church to the City Temple who eventually sold it to developers who demolished it in 1967 to erect Elmbank Chambers.

PARK PARISH CHURCH, LYNDOCH PLACE

*

Opened in 1857, J. T. Rochead's parish church was built for the Church of Scotland during the great age of church building. The interior was a different approach for a Church of Scotland building as it had a chancel, communion table, stained glass and no galleries.

When the church was demolished in 1969, the outcry was greater than for any other building in the city that had suffered a similar fate at the time. When the sale of the church had been announced three years previously, there was heated debate between the Church of Scotland and those who wanted to preserve the building. The main arguments focused on two questions. Did the owner of a historic building have the right to sell it for demolition and should a building of such importance within a larger area be preserved for the sake of that area? Despite the arguments and suggestions about other uses for the church, the demolition, except for the steeple, went ahead. Glasgow has long had a habit of retaining the steeple of buildings when the rest of the structure has been demolished, the Tolbooth, the Tron and the Merchants steeples being examples. Maybe it was seen as a compromise. The building of 1970 that replaced the church is out of keeping with its surroundings, which form part of the Park area, universally regarded as the finest example of Victorian planning in Britain.

Despite the church having no congregation – most of the buildings in the area had been converted to offices – how the Church of Scotland could have demolished such a fine church without finding another use for it is beyond

St Andrew's Free Church when it was reduced to housing a cash-and-carry concern.
To the left is an eighteenth-century mansion, although much altered. It, and all
the rest of the mansions once in the street, bar one, are now demolished.

comprehension. Greed must have overcome sentiment, as the site was very valuable.

St Andrew's Free Church, Charlotte Street

*

St Andrew's (later Trinity) Free Church was sandwiched between pedimented late-eighteenth-century mansions. Designed in 1862 by J. Honeyman, who specialised in church building, it had a three-gabled front, the centre projected with three lancets. Entrance to the church was by double-arched porches at the recessed aisle fronts, echoing the arcading of the base of the triple lancet gable of the nave. Internally, the church was spacious, with galleries supported

by cast-iron columns. It also had an outstanding hammer-beam ceiling.

Eventually the building became the property of the Central Church of Scotland and was used as the church halls for St Andrew's Parish Church. After many years of neglect, the building was demolished in 1984.

PUBLIC AND COMMERCIAL BUILDINGS

In the 1960s and 70s particularly and even into the 1980s, Glasgow's city planners were guilty of lunacy as they allowed scores of Victorian architectural gems to be demolished. For some reason Glasgow has always preferred to knock down the old to build the new, and this was very much the policy in the 1960s and 70s when the city fathers saw little merit in Victorian buildings and allowed them to be replaced by modern concrete eyesores. Fortunately, this attitude has now changed, but too late to save many beautiful buildings.

37–51 MILLER STREET
✳

Although Miller Street was laid out as a residential street, it was redeveloped as commercial premises rapidly from 1849. Its warehouses were unsurpassed, and on the west side of the street was the most sumptuous building ever erected for such a purpose. Venetian Renaissance in style, it was designed by Alexander Kirkland and built in 1854–6 for Anderson and Company. While the ground and first floors had a profusion of columns and Palladian windows with carved keystone heads along the street, the top floor formed a colonnade. Apart from the building being astonishingly elaborate for a warehouse, it was unusual in that the courtyard was open to the street, offering improved daytime lighting and special opportunities for spectacular architec-

Left.
This photograph shows the outside pulpit of Bridgegate Free Church, built in 1860 by architect J. J. Stevenson. It was one of two such pulpits, the other being outside MacDonald Free Church in Maitland Street, also Stevenson's work. The outside pulpit was so that the minister could preach to gatherings in the street. As the preachings were usually attacks on other persuasions, especially the Catholics, however, they led to rioting and obstructions in the street, resulting in the magistrates banning outside pulpits. The church was demolished in 1918 to make way for road widening. The steeple in the background is that of the old Merchant House.

37-51 Miller Street.

tural display, like sculpture in the spandrels, including some fine figures. The loading compartments were set back to the innermost bays where the combination of foreshortening and deep columnar relief practically hid them.

By the second half of the twentieth century, apart from the building being considered unsuitable for modern storage purposes, the once admired courtyard was deemed wasted space, and in 1969, after suffering from neglect, the building was pulled down. Of course there were protests, but, as usual, they were ignored, and Glasgow lost an incomparable example of Victorian architecture.

CORN EXCHANGE, HOPE STREET

*

Before the subway operations got in their way in the 1890s, farmers congregated in St Enoch Square each Wednesday. They then met in the Corn

The Corn Exchange, Hope Street.

Exchange, built in 1840 at the corner of Hope Street and Waterloo Street. The building was a high, single-storey hall with a Roman-Corinthian portico at the entrance. Although in 1858 an extension was added, it still did not make the building large enough, for in 1894 it was replaced by a larger building. Architect W. F. McGibbon was commissioned to design it, and the finished product was a very striking French Renaissance-style building with unusual columns made up of alternating square and circular drums, a feature repeated around the windows and even on the chimney-heads. The use of the square and circular drum treatment was particularly effective around the main doorway, which was two storeys in height and topped with something different for a Glasgow building, a broken pediment. Half-moon attic windows were set into the roof. There was nothing like the building in the city, but unfortunately, because of its closeness to Central Station, it became so blackened with soot that its exceptional features were obscured, and in 1963 it came into the hands of a property developer who, despite it being a listed building, demolished it soon afterwards.

CHRISTIAN INSTITUTE AND YMCA, BOTHWELL STREET

*

In 1873 a committee was formed with the purpose of providing an institute that would be the headquarters of the Young Men's Christian Association and a central meeting place for all bodies of a religious character. Five gentlemen giving £1,000 each headed the subscription list and in a short time £28,000 had been collected. Ground was purchased in Bothwell Street, and on it was erected a German Renaissance-style building designed by architect John McLeod. The building, opened by Lord Shaftsbury on 10 October 1879, was known as the Christian Institute. Mounted over the doorway were statues of John Knox and William Tyndale, and above the windows of the second floor were medallion busts of Martin Luther and other reformers. The cost, including site, building and furnishings, came to the enormous sum of £30,000.

In 1896 two wings were added to the building, creating the massive, but bizarre, pile shown in the illustration. Architect R. A. Bryden followed the exuberant style of the original building but added a different tall tower at each corner. (The finished building was pure fantasy, like a whimsical illustration from a Bavarian fairytale book.) The west wing contained a restaurant, a hostel with 195 beds for the YMCA, drawing, music, writing and smoking rooms. The east wing housed a Bible Training Institute with 100 bedrooms for male students and 50 for female students. There were also separate dining, writing and sitting rooms and libraries for each sex. The wings could not have been built if it had not been for the generosity of chemical manufacturer Lord Overton and his sister who provided much of the astronomical cost. The enlarged building, the total cost of which was a staggering £115,000, became the headquarters of the evangelical movement in the city.

By the 1960s the Christian Institute and the YMCA were struggling financially and finding it increasingly difficult to maintain their large, and internally awkward premises (floor and window levels varied). As a solution, a decision was made in 1974 to sell the centre and west parts of the building for redevelopment but to keep the east part, housing the Bible Training

Right.
Christian Institute and YMCA, Bothwell Street

Interior of the YMCA.

Institute belonging to the Glasgow Evangelistic Association. The plan, however, was turned down by the city planners, who said that any new development had to match the part retained, obviously an impossibility as it could never be replicated, even if anyone could have afforded to attempt it. Inevitably, the decision was made to demolish the whole building, which was done in the summer of 1980. Although many thought the building had no architectural merit, it was Glasgow's most fantastic building and its architecture was so over the top that it had a charm that was much missed.

THE SAILORS' HOME, BROOMIELAW

*

Most aerial views of the Broomielaw were taken from the lighthouse-like corner tower of the Sailors' Home. The call for a Sailors' Home, or hostel, first came up in 1853 when concern was felt that there was no suitable accommodation for the large numbers of seamen who stayed in the city while their ships were in port for loading, unloading and repair. Ambitious plans had

Right.
Robert Eadie's view of the Broomielaw showing the landmark campanile of the Sailors' Home.

R EADIE
26

been drawn up for such a building, but as there were insufficient funds to carry them out, a cheaper plan designed by J. T. Rochead was built in 1855–6. Rochead's plan might have been cheaper than the original, but it still cost £12,000 to fulfil. Situated a little west of the Clyde Port building, the Italianate four-storey Sailors' Home had a raised square tower at one end and, on the corner of James Watt Street rising to a height of six storeys, a circular campanile that became a well-known landmark and a welcoming one to visiting seamen. During reconstruction in 1906, an ugly mansard roof was added. When the Clyde ceased to be a major port the Home was closed and in 1971 it was demolished.

ST ANDREW'S HALLS, KENT ROAD, GRANVILLE AND BERKELEY STREETS
*

In 1875 a syndicate of wealthy west-end citizens who thought the City Hall in Candleriggs was inadequate, formed a company to provide halls in the west end of the city. A site at Kent Road, Granville Street and Berkeley Street was acquired, and two years later a building containing a large main hall with adjoining smaller halls had been completed at a cost of £101,000. The architect was James Sellars, and the new St Andrew's Halls, as they were named, were his masterpiece.

A colonnaded upper storey resting on a heavy channelled masonry plinth dominated the frontage to Granville Street. Incorporated into the plinth were four giant pedestals supporting sculptured groups by John Mossman. Atlantis divided the central doors. Above the main cornice were attic storeys, the outer bays of which contained caryatids referring to the arts. Those to the north were inscribed RAPHAEL, WATT, M-ANGELO, NEWTON and FLAXMAN. To the south were PURCELL, BACH, HANDEL, MOZART and BEETHOVEN. The powerful classical frontage was matched by the interior. No expense was spared in its decoration, particularly the concert hall, capable of holding 4,500 people. It had galleries on three sides and a projecting platform that made sure that members of the audience had a perfect view no matter where they were seated. Acoustically, the hall was perfect and it had one of the finest organs in the land. In 1890 the city purchased St Andrew's Halls for £37,500 and then spent over £6,000 in improving it.

As well as being used for musical performances, the building hosted political meetings and, in 1902, was the venue for the first general assembly of the recently constituted United Free Church. The Glasgow Choral Union often

St Andrew's Halls, Kent Road, Granville and Berkeley Streets.

performed in the halls, as did many of the world's greatest musical performers, like the Italian tenor Enrico Caruso who sang there on 3 September 1909.

It was a non-musical event that led to the building's demise. On the evening of 26 October 1962, a boxing match had been held in the main hall. By 5 a.m. on the 27th the building was on fire and by morning only the blackened walls remained. Afterwards the fire chief wrote: 'From a fire-fighting point of view, the blaze was one of the saddest encountered in the long history of the service, for there disappeared a building which had been an integral part of the day to day life of the citizens of Glasgow.'

Although St Andrew's Halls were not rebuilt, they were not entirely lost to the city. During 1972–80 the Granville Street facade was restored and the interior of the front part reconstructed to form the Mitchell Theatre. The rear was rebuilt as an extension to the Mitchell Library.

GRAND HOTEL,
CHARING CROSS
*

When the Grand Hotel was built in 1878 it was the most opulent and fashionable hotel in town. It was designed by architect James Brown in French style and would not have looked out of place in Paris. The Grand's superiority was short-lived, however, as when the railway companies built their opulent hotels alongside their city centre stations it was considered to be too far away from the stations. Nevertheless, despite the loss of its crown, the Grand was popular for wedding receptions and dances, and as it was convenient for the west-end theatres and concert rooms, it was in demand with those frequenting such places. During the Second World War the American Red Cross took over the Grand as a club for US Forces on leave in Scotland. After the war the hotel became shabby and impossible to run, and in early 1969 it was demolished to make way for the M8 motorway and finished up as rubble used as infill for the obsolete dry dock at Meadowside. Although many thought its demolishment was unnecessary, it allowed the magnificent Charing Cross Mansions to dominate Charing Cross.

ST ENOCH HOTEL,
ST ENOCH SQUARE
*

One of the worst cases of lunacy by the planning department in the 1970s was the demolishment of a Grand Hotel rival, the St Enoch Hotel, built for the Glasgow and South Western Railway in 1875–79. Behind was a station with a magnificent arched train shed similar to that of St Pancras in London but smaller. The shed was the first public area in Glasgow to be lit by electricity. John Fowler and J. F. Blair designed the station, which was opened by the Prince of Wales on 17 October 1876, at which time the northern range of offices and the hotel had not been built. In 1900 an extension to the south side added six platforms, making a total of fourteen.

When the stupendous Gothic pile designed by Thomas Willson that was the St Enoch Hotel opened on 3 July 1879 it was regarded as the 'most imposing structure in Glasgow', and with 200 bedrooms, 20 public rooms and a staff of 80 it was the largest hotel in Scotland and the third largest in Europe. The main frontage on the east of St Enoch Square was 360 feet long and 120

Left.
Grand Hotel, Charing Cross.

ST. ENOCH STATION. GLASGOW.

St Enoch Hotel, St Enoch Square.

feet high and the northern wing extended from St Enoch Square to Dunlop Street. Running across the frontage was a terraced carriageway with a central iron and glass veranda with four doorways leading to the main booking office. Shops and refreshment bars occupied the Gothic arches supporting the terrace. The station was entered through the arches and guests could enter the hotel via a groined open porch at the foot of the carriageway.

Despite the luxurious public rooms, the lavish bedrooms, the excellent service and cuisine, by 1910 St Enoch's had been surpassed by the Central Hotel, which had double the number of rooms and staff. Although the Central had become the city's number one hotel, St Enoch's was still a favourite with those who preferred quieter surroundings, and it was the headquarters of most of the Ayrshire and south country lairds when they visited the city. During the Second World War the hotel was the headquarters of Naval Intelligence.

Although the station was closed in 1966 and its traffic transferred to the Central, the hotel stayed open until 1974 when it was closed because it did not comply with new fire regulations. Despite an outcry and last-ditch attempts to save the well-known landmark, the hotel was demolished in 1975, suppos-

Botanic Gardens Station, Great Western Road.

edly to make way for a huge office block to house Civil Service jobs being transferred from London. This plan never materialised and eventually the giant St Enoch Centre shopping centre was built on the site. People still talk affectionately about the hotel and how it was a disgrace it was knocked down and that at least the facade should have been retained.

BOTANIC GARDENS STATION,
GREAT WESTERN ROAD
*

Among railway stations lost to Glasgow was Botanic Gardens, somewhat smaller than St Enoch's but sadly missed for its picturesque appearance. The station was part of the Caledonian Railway's Glasgow Central (low level) line, begun in 1890. The Glasgow Central Railway passed under some of the busiest streets of the city and among its twelve stations were Bridgeton Cross, Glasgow Green, Glasgow Cross, Glasgow Central, Kelvingrove and Botanic Gardens. Some of the stations had buildings at two levels, but at

Botanic Gardens the only building was at ground level.

A particular feature of the Caledonian Railway Company's stations was that they were all eye-catching and designed by specialist architects who also worked for rival companies. James Miller began working for Caledonian Railway in 1888 and his 'Arts and Crafts'-style station buildings were popular with the travelling public. His station at Botanic Gardens (1893) was one of his most fanciful designs, with an Oriental flavour, and at the time was described as 'a strange sight in Glasgow'. Although it had the, by then, familiar half-timbered gables and red-brick walls, it had a veranda in front and, what gave it its Oriental look, two tall towers on the roof capped with balconies and golden onion-shaped domes. It also had four tall chimneys that balanced the towers. Miller's delightful station provided a bit of light relief in an area full of solid Victorian buildings and when it was demolished in 1970 following a fire, it was much missed.

DEPARTMENT STORES

Next to London, Glasgow had more department stores than any other city in Britain. In fact, it was a Glasgow man, John Anderson, who took credit for the concept of 'universal trading', a store with various departments. Among the department stores once in the city were Lewis's, Paisley's, Dalys, Trerons, The Colosseum, Arnotts, McDonalds, Wylie and Lochhead, Wylie Hill, Copland and Lye, Pettigrew and Stephens, Frasers and Watt Brothers. Of these, only Watt Brothers and Frasers remain. Although all but two of the stores have gone, four of their buildings have survived. Two of those that have not belonged to the rival stores Copland and Lye and Pettigrew and Stephens, who were neighbours in Sauchiehall Street and whose buildings ended their days simultaneously as they were demolished, in the face of severe condemnation, to make way for the Sauchiehall Street Centre.

COPLAND AND LYE, CALEDONIAN HOUSE, SAUCHIEHALL STREET
*

The earlier of the rival stores was Copland and Lye, founded by William Copland and John Lye in 1873. It had started in Cowcaddens but in five years

Right.
Copland and Lye, Caledonian House, Sauchiehall Street.

Copland and Lye's magnificent wrought-iron staircase and galleried interior in 1922.
The photograph must have been taken in summer as parasols, swimming costumes
and straw hats are on display.

had grown so much that it moved into new premises in Sauchiehall Street, Glasgow's up-and-coming shopping street. Designed by James Boucher, the new store, named Caledonian House, was described as 'one of the most extensive, most architecturally elegant and the most perfectly equipped drapery emporiums to be met with in the kingdom'. An idea of the vast development of the firm's business can be formed from the fact that instead of the twenty assistants it first employed, by the end of the 1880s it had around 400. The major contributor to this success was the following philosophy written into the firm's brochure and staff manual: 'Good merchandise is useless without good service . . . Small transactions well executed lead to big ones.'

While the French Renaissance exterior of Caledonian House, which was remodelled and extended in the 1890s, was imposing, the galleried interior was no less so. The spectacular stairwell gave splendid views of lofty well-lighted departments displaying every kind of drapery imaginable. Like most department stores, Copland's had a tearoom-restaurant with music provided by the company's own musical ensemble. It was said the recipe for Copland's famed pineapple cakes remained unchanged for almost 100 years.

Copland and Lye was one of the few stores in the city not to become part of the House of Fraser. It belonged to the Ogg family, who are still in the business but in a smaller establishment in Milngavie. Although Caledonian House was demolished in 1973 to make way for the Sauchiehall Street Centre, the store had closed some time before as by the end of the 1960s department stores were finding it difficult to survive as their overheads were astronomical and shopping habits had changed.

PETTIGREW AND STEPHENS, MANCHESTER HOUSE, SAUCHIEHALL STREET
*

Pettigrew and Stephens was founded in 1888 at the corner of Sauchiehall Street and West Campbell Street. Like Copland and Lye, it was rapidly successful thanks to Andrew Pettigrew who was in sole charge after the early death of his partner, W. H. Stephens. Pettigrew had started in the business in 1875 at the age of eighteen, and among the stores he had worked for was Copland and Lye, twice. By the first half of the 1890s Pettigrew and Stephens had expanded into adjoining property and a tearoom had been opened in Manchester House, the name by which Pettigrew and Stephens' premises was known.

A major rebuilding/refurbishment, begun in 1896, created a French Renaissance building like Copland's but more sophisticated. John Keppie was the architect and his building featured a gilt dome originally designed by his assistant, Charles Rennie Mackintosh, for a chapterhouse. Internally, the building was divided into three bays of galleries, and standing on the ground floor gave an uninterrupted view right up to the top storey, the roof of which was fitted with an abundance of glass that lit up the whole interior. Grecian marble adorned the walls of the main staircase and the windows were fitted with stained glass.

The rebuilt store opened in May 1901 with seven floors of departments, ranging from silks to confectionery and carpets to china. There were also tearooms and reading rooms. The company's advertising material stated: 'No such shopping centre where the whole wants of the family can be supplied, exists in Scotland.'

PETTIGREW & STEPHENS.

Pettigrew and Stephens continued to expand and in 1909 took over J. J. Burnet's splendid Fine Art Institute lying between it and Copland and Lye. The Fine Art Institute was demolished after a fire in 1967, and in 1973 Pettigrew and Stephens and Copland and Lye were demolished, robbing Sauchiehall Street in the space of six years of three of its landmark buildings.

The House of Fraser, who owned Pettigrew & Stephens, had decided in 1970 to close the store, demolish it and open a new House of Fraser store within a shopping complex on the Pettigrew and Stephens' site. Planning permission was refused, and in 1971, to reinforce its position, the House of Fraser acquired the site of the closed Copland and Lye store. In 1974 the ugly Sauchiehall Street Centre was built on the site of both stores. People still talk nostalgically about Copland and Lye's and Pettigrew and Stephens' fine buildings and how disgraceful it was that they were demolished and replaced with a development of little architectural merit.

INTERIORS

Some of Glasgow's landmark buildings that had become obsolete commercially were saved from demolition by retaining the exterior and gutting the interior. While this can be appreciated along the lines of half a loaf is better than none, it is a shame that as a result interiors that matched, and often surpassed, the splendour of the exteriors have gone. Two such cases are the former Western Club in Buchanan Street and the former Grosvenor Restaurant in Gordon Street. It was not only buildings of great architectural merit that had spectacular interiors, however; some, like those in the Crown Lunch and Tea Rooms in Argyle Street, were in commonplace buildings.

FORMER WESTERN CLUB, BUCHANAN STREET

*

The former Western Club at 147 Buchanan Street was the work of David and James Hamilton. Begun in 1839, it was an early example of Italianate architecture in Glasgow and one of the finest Victorian buildings in the country. John Honeyman added an extension in 1870. Internally the building was palatial, with a Corinthian pillared hall and a vast, stately staircase that branched

Left.
Pettigrew and Stephens, Manchester House, Sauchiehall Street.

Western Club's Corinthian pillared hall and main staircase with its magnificent stained-glass window and massive gilt lamp on the first landing.

to the left and right. On the first landing a magnificent stained-glass window provided a backdrop for a massive gilt lamp with five lanterns. As befitted such an elitist establishment, the huge public rooms were luxurious.

By the beginning of the 1960s, the club was no longer convenient or economic, and the decision was taken to sell the building to a developer who wanted to demolish it. There was an outcry, and an article in the *Architect's Journal* in 1962, signed by someone calling himself 'Astragal', said how serious the loss would be of the Western Club, David Hamilton's final masterpiece and one of the finest early Victorian buildings in the county. The outcome was that after intervention by, of all bodies, Glasgow Corporation, David Hamilton's facade was retained but John Honeyman's extension was demolished and replaced by an office block. Hamilton's building was gutted inside, and today The Pier occupies it. While it is sad that all its internal splendour has gone, it is good that such an important building has a new lease of life.

*Interior of the Grosvenor Restaurant's spectacular banqueting hall with
sculptures designed by notable Glasgow sculptor Albert Hodge who, having trained
as an architect, was especially aware of the correct proportions of sculptured
figures in relation to the area they were ornamenting.*

GROSVENOR RESTAURANT,
74 GORDON STREET
*

The building known to Glaswegians for decades as the Grosvenor Restaurant
began as a warehouse built speculatively by the firm of Alexander and
George Thomson in 1859–61. Consisting of a basement and three storeys
topped by a deeply recessed consoled eaves gallery, it burnt down in 1866 but
was rebuilt to the same design.

When William McKillop took over the ground and first floors as a
restaurant in the 1890s, he altered the street-level frontage and added a
magnificent marble staircase leading to the upper floor previously occupied
as offices. Further alterations came in 1902–07 when J. H. Craigie of Clarke

and Bell added an ungainly two storeys with twin baroque domes. At the same time, the old second and third floors were combined to create a spectacular German baroque banqueting hall. The marble staircase was also extended and ornamented with sculptured figures and stained glass. Ornate plaster and woodwork concealed the structural steelwork in the double-height banqueting hall, and exceptionally fine eye-level caryatids supported the curved roof beams. Magnificent chandeliers provided the lighting. After the alterations, the Grosvenor was Glasgow's most sumptuous restaurant and rivalled the Grand Hotel as the rendezvous of the young set.

Half a century later the Grosvenor was again altered. Edwardian splendour was out and Fifties style in. In 1959, the marble staircase was taken out and the interior was modernised, a desecration not everyone approved of, as is clear from an account by a *Glasgow Herald* reporter on what he called this 'melancholy but inspiring occasion'. 'The old restaurant with its marble pillars and curlicues did not merely belong to Glasgow, it was a period piece of which all Britain could be proud. Its loss is severe.' He did go on to say that 'the new Grosvenor rises gloriously, like Venus from the sea and in elegance, comfort and mood will hold its own against anything the rest of the country can offer'.

As the popularity of the formal functions for which the Grosvenor catered declined, the restaurant closed, and after a fire in the late 1960s the building was reconstructed as offices behind the facade, removing the last vestiges of the spectacular interiors. Five of the magnificent chandeliers ended up in the Trades Hall in Glassford Street.

CROWN LUNCH AND TEA ROOMS, 114 ARGYLE STREET

✳

Although just as special, nothing could be more different from the palatial interiors of the Western Club and the Grosvenor than the interior of the Crown Lunch and Tea Rooms. The building still stands and was a wedding present from Major John Cochrane to his bride, Miss Catherine Cranston. It was a plain late-eighteenth-century tenement that Miss Cranston refronted and remodelled into the Crown Lunch and Tea Rooms in 1897.

The interior was by George Walton, helped by Charles Rennie Mackintosh who designed the first of his innovative high-backed chairs for the lunch room. Innovative though Walton's work was, however, the most famous interior at Argyle Street was the basement Dutch Kitchen designed

Mackintosh's Dutch Kitchen, showing inglenook fireplace, black beams and black and white checked linoleum with ceramic tiling in a smaller black and white checked pattern marking off the inglenook area.

by Mackintosh in 1906. Whether it was his idea or Miss Cranston's of what a Dutch kitchen should look like, the only Dutch feel to it was a delft-tiled fireplace with a rack for decorative plates above a large fake inglenook area. The rest of the decor was strikingly different. The ceiling was black, black columns half-screened the ingle, and the floor was covered with black and white checked linoleum. Above the dado, the walls were sparkling white, and although Mackintosh had chosen traditional Windsor style for his chairs, they were emerald green. A little pink in the weeping rose detail in the leaded windows was the only other touch of colour. The result was vibrant urban style, not country Dutch.

Subsequent owners of the building gradually removed all traces of Walton's and Mackintosh's fine interiors until nothing remained. It has to be remembered, however, that around the 1950s work by people like Walton and Mackintosh was considered old-hat, as everyone wanted shiny modern interiors not pseudo old-fashioned Dutch decor.

EXHIBITIONS

Following the success of the Crystal Palace exhibition in London in 1851, other cities began to stage their own grand international exhibitions, like Paris in 1867 and, nearer home, Edinburgh in 1886 and Manchester in 1887. Glasgow took the plunge in 1888 with the first of its five major exhibitions. The others were in 1901, 1911, 1938 and 1988.

Only the 1888 exhibition truly falls within the Victorian age, but as the 1901 exhibition was conceived in 1897 and took place in the year of Victoria's death, it is permissible to include it in the Victorian City section of *Lost Glasgow*.

1888 INTERNATIONAL EXHIBITION

*

Glasgow decided to hold an international exhibition in 1888 to raise funds to build an art gallery, museum and school of art to house under one roof the city's art collection displayed in the McLellan Galleries and its historical, scientific and technical collections exhibited in Kelvingrove House. Another aim was to 'promote and foster the sciences and the arts, and to stimulate commercial enterprise'. The site chosen for the Glasgow International Exhibition of Science and Art was Kelvingrove Park, the main building located approximately where the Art Gallery now stands.

Architect James Sellars won the competition to design the Exhibition buildings, which were Oriental in style, a mixture of Moorish, Indian and Byzantine, with many domes and minarets. In Glasgow, the Exhibition was known as 'Baghdad on the Kelvin'. On 8 May, the Prince and Princess of Wales drove to Kelvingrove where the Prince declared the Exhibition open by unlocking the main building, a splendid 'Eastern Palace', with a golden key. On 22 August, Queen Victoria arrived for a state visit and two days later returned for a private visit.

The chief feature of the Exhibition was an impressive representation of the bygone Bishop's Castle, which contained a spectacular collection of Scottish antiquities. For the younger generation who were maybe not quite so interested in history nearby was a switchback railway that ran along the

Panoramic view of the 1888 International Exhibition at Kelvingrove Park.
The L-shaped building in the foreground is Kelvingrove House with its additions.
To the right of the Exhibition building is the Machinery Court.

north bank of the River Kelvin in front of the University grounds. It was a breathtaking novelty and the Exhibition's best-loved attraction. Those with a weaker constitution could sail on the Kelvin in a real Venetian gondola.

Entertainments included a military tournament, music by various bands, firework displays, cycling carnivals, football matches and swimming galas held in the Kelvin. The fairy fountain with its many-coloured jets was the finest display of water and illumination ever seen in Scotland.

Most of the activities were under the roof of the main building, and besides local and Scottish exhibitors there were courts from Burma, Canada, Ceylon, India, France, Germany, Holland, plus other countries. Very popular was the Machinery Court, and 'Women's Industries', where home industries and crafts were demonstrated, was well attended. Unsurprisingly, with the Clyde's background of shipbuilding, the Naval Architecture and Marine Engineering Department with its lavish display of ship models was always busy.

Catering for the vast crowds was on a large scale, and among the many offerings were the pricey Royal Bungalow, the Bachelor's Café, the Bodega, and the Indian and the Ceylon Tearooms with native waiters. The

The representation of the bygone Bishop's Castle, a prime attraction of the Exhibition,
which stood on the University side of the river, separated from the main building.
Sellars had reconstructed it from contemporary drawings and while it might have
looked realistic, it was simply a wooden frame covered with canvas inventively painted.

Temperance Movement was acknowledged, and the large Bishop's Palace
Temperance Café, run by J. Lyons, had waitresses in Mary Queen of Scots
outfits. Also offering non-alcoholic refreshment was Van Houten's sixteenth-
century-style Cocoa House, the most artistic building in the grounds. Inside
it was furnished with Dutch antiques and girls in national dress served cocoa
at two shillings a cup.

When the Exhibition closed in November, 5,746,179 people had visited it
and takings amounted to £225, 928 15s 2d, leaving a surplus of £46,000.

After the Exhibition, all the buildings, mostly constructed of wood, were
demolished. The only reminder was the spectacular terracotta Doulton
Fountain that stood outside the main building. The fountain was the main
Doulton exhibit and Sir Henry Doulton presented it to the city, which moved

View of the Exhibition from the University. The building to the right beside the trees is Miss Cranston's Tea House. In the centre is the Industrial Hall with its grand central dome, gilded and topped with the figure of light. The piazza between the facade of the central dome and the colonnade was a popular place for people to congregate.

it to Glasgow Green where it still is, but in a vandalised state. Plans are in place to restore it.

1901 INTERNATIONAL EXHIBITION
✳

As the profits of the 1888 Exhibition had been more than doubled by public subscription and the Corporation had given part of the Kelvingrove site, the Association for the Promotion of Art launched a competition in 1891 for the design of a new municipal art gallery and museum, a purpose of the Exhibition. The plans were meant to include a concert hall and a school of art but both were dropped later because of lack of funds. From the 62 designs

Beneath the Dome. The illustration shows sculptures by Albert Hodge with, in pride of place, an eighteen-foot statue of the new king, Edward VII, the first to be raised in his honour. While the statue of the king was not highly rated, the figures depicting 'The Triumph of Navigation' were admired. Figures on ships' prows dominate the corners.

submitted, that of John W. Simpson and E. J. Miller Allan was selected. When the Duke of York laid the foundation stone in 1897, it seemed a good idea to organise a second exhibition to inaugurate the building.

The architect chosen to design the 1901 exhibition, opened on 2 May by Princess Louise, Duchess of Fife, was James Miller whose striking buildings spread over 73 acres of Kelvingrove Park and its surroundings (the Exhibition was known in Glasgow as 'the Groveries'). The site was a wonderland of domed and towered pavilions conceived by Miller as Spanish Renaissance but considered more Oriental than Spanish in appearance by Glaswegians. Miller's choice of design was to harmonise with the centrepiece of the Exhibition, the new Art Gallery and Museum.

The Machinery Hall was where the Kelvin Hall now stands and a sports stadium with grandstands was laid out in the University grounds. Among the outstanding attractions were the main building, the Industrial Hall, with its magnificent golden dome topped by a Statue of Light, the Fine Art Section in the new Art Galleries and the Grand Concert Hall. Motor car trials, a fantastic water chute, and the switchback railway so popular in 1888 provided relaxation.

Among the countries with pavilions in the grounds were Canada, France and Ireland. Russia had more space than any other country and the 'Russian Village' had six buildings, four of them magnificent pavilions after the style of ancient northern Russian houses. Local department stores like Pettigrew and Stephens, Copland and Lye, and Wylie and Lochead exhibited in the Industrial Hall, and in the Machinery Hall names like Water Macfarlane, Fairfield's, Colville's and Beardmore appeared.

As with the 1888 Exhibition, catering was on a vast scale. The upmarket Royal Bungalow had returned, as had Van Houten's, this time in 'Old English' style, not traditional Dutch. A newcomer was Miss Cranston's Tea House, the top floor an open creeper-shaded Terrace Tea Garden. Flint's Tea Rooms near the Concert Hall rivalled Miss Cranston's.

One of the best-remembered things about the Exhibition was the electric tramcar. The first had been introduced in 1898, and it was the aim to have the service all-electric by the opening of the Exhibition. This was achieved and few people walked to Kelvingrove in 1901 as there were 332 trams running.

The success of the Exhibition, running from 2 May to 9 November, was remarkable, with even the weather being considerate. Intended to illustrate the growth of art, industry and science during the previous century, it was the largest exhibition so far held in Britain and the profit of £40,000 went towards restoring the Park and acquiring exhibits for Glasgow's new Art Galleries, which did not open officially to the public until 25 October 1902.

All that survived from the Exhibition was a fountain, relocated to Alexandra Park, and the delightful Sunlight Cottages, modelled on one of the blocks of houses at Lever Brothers' model township of Port Sunlight in Cheshire. A reprehensible decision had been made to demolish Kelvingrove House to make room for the Exhibition, a deed made worse when the extension was retained and converted into the Japan Pavilion.

APPENDIX

*

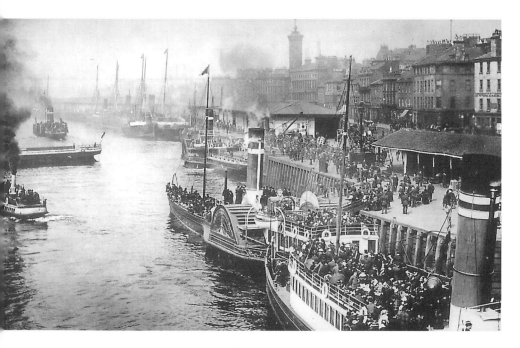

BROOMIELAW

*

This photograph shows a scene long lost to Glasgow, a bustling Broomielaw and a River Clyde teeming with shipping. The crowded paddle steamers in the foreground are bound 'doon the watter' to Clyde resorts such as Dunoon, Rothesay and Arran. At the height of summer forty to fifty steamers a day left the Broomielaw. The steamers on the quay behind sailed to Ireland. On the left is one of the Clutha waterbuses, which operated on the river for the three miles between Victoria Bridge and Whiteinch Ferry. They carried around 300 passengers at a penny a time and called at landing stages on either bank, the whole journey taking about forty-five minutes. The tower in the background belonged to the Sailors' Home. Most of the buildings lining this part of the Broomielaw have been demolished and replaced, and a river walkway takes the place of the old sheds of the busy Steamboat Quay.

THE LOST STREET

*

The west side of Jamaica Street looking north, *c.* 1880s. Only one of the buildings in the photograph remains, and what makes this scene particularly sad is that some of the lost buildings were a reminder of Glasgow's great engineering past as they were constructed of cast-iron and glass, a type of architecture that Glasgow pioneered. Jamaica Street was famous for its collection of early iron-framed warehouses. The building on the right is the only remaining one. Known as 'The Iron Building', it was built for the furniture firm of Gardner's and was the first and finest of the street's great iron edifices. Designed in 1855 by John Baird with iron work by ironfounder R. McConnell, who held the patent for the wrought- and cast-iron beams, it was famous for being the first everyday building in which the lessons of the Crystal Palace's prefabricated structure were successfully applied. Among other buildings in the street with cast-iron facades were those belonging to Paisleys and the Colosseum (the main block).

The east side of Jamaica Street looking north, *c.* 1880s. Not one of the buildings on the left of the photograph remains. Note R. W. Forsyth's shop on the corner of Howard Street. Later it moved to the corner of Gordon Street and Renfield Street. The street was just as busy in the 1880s as it is today, except that the traffic was two-way and the vehicles rather different – horse-drawn omnibuses, carts and vans. With its cabbie resplendent in a top hat, cab licence number 645 sits outside the Colosseum store.

McGeoch's Building
*

While Glasgow is essentially a Victorian city, the classical tradition was perpetuated into the Edwardian age, the 1920s and the 1930s by architects such as James Miller, John A. Campbell and J. J. Burnet, described in 1923 as 'the greatest British architect of the present time'. From the age of seventeen, Burnet, the son of Glasgow architect John Burnet senior, studied at the Ecole des Beaux-Arts in Paris. On returning to Glasgow in 1877, he joined his father's firm and started his career with an exceptional design for the Fine Art Institute in Sauchiehall Street (1879), which showed the influence of his Paris training. When selected to design the Edward VII Gallery at the British Museum in 1903, Burnet moved his main office from Glasgow to London. For his outstanding work, he was knighted in 1914.

McGeoch Building.

Of Burnet's twenty-five buildings in Glasgow, the warehouse for iron-mongers William McGeoch and Company at the corner of Cadogan Street and West Campbell Street, which he designed in 1905, was his most impressive and experimental building in the city. Inspired by the tall modern office blocks seen by Burnet during a visit to America in 1896, it had Classical and Beaux-Arts elements that blended perfectly. Behind the huge building's stone facade was a steel frame supporting some of the first reinforced concrete slabs to be cast in Britain *in situ*. (Burnet had studied the new steel-framed structures while in America and had used them in 1899 in his Atlantic Chambers, Hope Street, and Waterloo Chambers, Waterloo Street). As McGeoch's building was an outstanding example of Edwardian architecture and the finest of its type in the city, it was inexcusable and a needless loss when, despite protest, it was demolished in 1971.

THE ALHAMBRA THEATRE
✳

The exceptional J. J. Burnet was also the architect of the Alhambra Theatre in Waterloo Street. It was the only theatre designed by him and was large, with 2,750 seats and all modern innovations including a revolving stage. Its

The Alhambra Theatre.

opening on 9 December 1910 was an elegant occasion, with sightseers turning out to watch the first-night crowd dressed in their evening finery arrive in chauffeur-driven cars. The Alhambra functioned as an upmarket music hall until 1926 when it began staging operas, plays, musical comedies and revues featuring the biggest stars in show business. The Alhambra pantomimes with Harry Gordon and Will Fyffe were the best in the city, and the lavish *Five Past Eight* revues were hugely popular. Two Royal Variety Shows were held in the theatre.

In 1954 the Alhambra became the property of Howard and Wyndham, who also owned the King's and the Royal. By the 1960s, however, Howard and Wyndham could no longer maintain three theatres in the city, and in 1966 they sold the King's to Glasgow Corporation and in 1969 sold the Alhambra to developers. The theatre closed in May 1969 and, despite a petition signed by 500,000 people and the fact that at the time it was the only listed theatre in the city, it was demolished in 1971, the same year as the McGeoch building, and replaced by a nondescript office block. (1971 was a black year in Glasgow for buildings being demolished.)

The Regent Cinema, Renfield Street,
during refurbishment in 1937.

THE REGENT CINEMA
∗

Just outside the Edwardian era, the Regent, or the Cinema Picture House as it was initially called, opened in December 1911 and over its lifetime underwent a few changes. The original Regency-style facade was one storey high and the auditorium had just over 600 seats. In 1920 an extra storey with a bay window was added, at which time the cinema was renamed the Regent and had seating for 1,314. Another extension and revamp came in 1937 and a final refurbishment in 1971 after a fire in June.

Between the World Wars the Regent was a popular cinema, often sharing the opening of new films with the larger venues. Although after the Second World War it was overshadowed by the nearby Paramount (later the Odeon), the Regent held its own despite usually showing second-run films. Eventually, however, this was to become its downfall and even though it continued to attract loyal customers after the refurbishment of 1971, the cinema closed in 1982 and soon after was demolished and replaced with an office block called Regent House.

*The Exhibition's largest building, the Palace of Industry, which was temporarily
retained after the Exhibition to house the Scottish Motor Exhibition.*

1911 Exhibition

✳

Also just outside the Edwardian era was Glasgow's third great exhibition, the
Scottish Exhibition of National History, Art and Industry, which took place
in 1911. Its aim was to raise funds to endow a Chair of Scottish History and
Literature in Glasgow University. Unlike the International Exhibitions of
1888 and 1901, that of 1911 was national, with its emphasis on Scotland.
Kelvingrove Park was again the venue, but this time the exhibition site was
to the east end of the park, leaving the Museum and Art Gallery off limits.

Exhibits were housed in 'Palaces' – History, Industry, Art, Electrical and
Engineering, Music, and Decorative Arts. There were also various lesser
pavilions and kiosks. The main building was the vast steel-framed, asbestos-
covered Palace of History, modelled on Falkland Palace.

On the west bank of the River Kelvin, opposite the Palace of History,
was the 'Auld Toun', a mock burghal town characterising quaint bits of old
Scottish architecture. While the turreted and crow-stepped buildings looked
authentic, they were actually constructed of wood, plaster and cleverly

Postcard showing the Highland 'Clachan'.

painted canvas. Guarding the Toun was the Old Castle Keep, which camou-
flaged the Saracen Fountain, given to the city after the 1901 Exhibition and
later moved to Alexandra Park. In the Toun, old houses from Glasgow's
Stockwell Street, High Street, Rottenrow and Gorbals were represented, as
was St Ninian's Chapel and Old Gorbals Tower. The main square had a
mercat cross, the 'Auld Tartan Shop' and the 'Olde Toffee Shoppe'. There was
a town crier, and employees were dressed in 'old-fashioned' costume. The
Auld Toun was intended to kindle the imagination of the onlooker and to give
reality and a vivid setting to history and historical scenes. Visitors could
dream that suddenly they had been transported into the life and manners of
bygone centuries.

Noteworthy in the amusement area was an aerial railway conveying
passengers across the Kelvin, 130 feet up, in a car suspended from a metal diri-
gible electrically propelled along cables. A strange feature of the amusement
area, and hugely popular, were displays of members of native races living in
mock-ups of their 'ethnic' habitats. Scotland's own 'aborigines' were displayed
in the 'Clachan', a Highland village on the banks of the Caol Abhain (the River
Kelvin). All the Clachan's employees were Gaelic-speaking Highlanders.

The Exhibition opened on 3 May and closed on 4 November. The
weather was the best in living memory. There were only twelve bad days, two
of them the opening and closing days. During the 160 days of its existence,
9,369,375 people visited the Exhibition and £15,000 of the profit was set aside
to endow a Chair of Scottish History.

INDEX

✳

Illustrations appearing in the book are highlighted in bold type.